Edward Norris Kirk, John Waddington

Track of the Hidden Church

The Springs of the Pilgrim Movement

Edward Norris Kirk, John Waddington

Track of the Hidden Church
The Springs of the Pilgrim Movement

ISBN/EAN: 9783337293345

Printed in Europe, USA, Canada, Australia, Japan

Cover: Foto ©Lupo / pixelio.de

More available books at **www.hansebooks.com**

TRACK

OF THE

HIDDEN CHURCH;

OR, THE

SPRINGS OF THE PILGRIM MOVEMENT

BY

JOHN WADDINGTON, D. D.

PASTOR OF THE CHURCH OF THE PILGRIM FATHERS, SOUTHWARK, ENG.

WITH AN INTRODUCTION
BY
REV. E. N. KIRK, D. D.

BOSTON:
CONGREGATIONAL BOARD OF PUBLICATION,
13 CORNHILL.

Entered according to Act of Congress in the year 1863, by
THE CONGREGATIONAL BOARD OF PUBLICATION,
in the Clerk's Office of the District Court of Massachusetts.

CAMBRIDGE: ALLEN AND FARNHAM.

PREFACE.

On the eve of my departure from America, the request was made, at a meeting held in Mount Vernon Chapel, Boston, that immediately after my return to my native land, I should put in some connected form the facts which I had communicated to large assemblies in the course of my tour through the Northern States and in Canada.

Suggestions of the kind made previously by friends, in whose judgment I had confidence, prepared me to yield obedience to this valedictory injunction. The result is in this Memorial volume. I cannot promise myself that it will meet the expectation of the beloved and honored brethren who imposed the duty upon me, but they will accept it as the simple tribute of grateful attachment.

Very pleasant and refreshing are my recollections of New England, and of New England families in other States.

Every day my thoughts revert to them with an interest which a stranger cannot understand. If the story of our martyrs, in relation to that of the Pilgrims, should gain the attention of the young people of America, and tend to inspire new devotedness in the cause of truth and freedom, my satisfaction in the visit will be complete.

My aim has been to give the heart-life of these ancient worthies,— and to allow them to tell their own experience.

Ecclesiastical history is usually written after the model of the Book of Kings. We want rather a narrative more like the the Acts of the Apostles. On a careful consideration of the facts contained in this historical sketch, it will be seen that the Pilgrim Fathers were neither Brownists nor Puritans, properly so called. Discrimination on this point would prevent much misdirected reproach, and render needless apologies that are offered for acts committed by a different order of men.

It has strangely happened that writers in England, most conversant with outside particulars of

Pilgrim history, have shown the least acquaintance with their principles and spirit. They have gratified an antiquarian curiosity at the expense of the men of whom the world was not worthy. The best vindication of their fame is to spend some time, so far as it is possible, in their company, — reading their letters, or listening to their conversation.

Many who read these pages will be solicitous to know something of the prospects of the Memorial Church. It is already known that the church formed by Henry Jacob, in 1616, continues in existence. A few years ago the place of worship, occupied by the society, was lost to it from the lapse of the lease. The church, without a permanent home, amidst the dissipating influences of London, was in great danger of becoming extinct. The Hon. Abbott Lawrence enjoined the pastor to stand by the flock, in the assurance that the descendants of the Pilgrims in America would strengthen his hands to erect a Memorial Church in commemoration of the Pilgrims. For three years after vacating their home, the church could obtain no site on which to build. Their object was discouraged and opposed. It would require a separate volume to recount their trials and difficulties. Last year I ventured across the Atlantic to tell the circumstances of the case. The financial success of the visit was not sufficient to warrant us to attempt the completion of the building; but it enabled us to meet the claims of the builder, the architect, and solicitor for the erection of a portion of the structure, a part of which is occupied for public worship by the church, and another part as a school-room. It will interest our friends to know that, to the extent of our accommodation, the congregation has increased. Necessarily, however, without further enlargement, its resources would be inadequate to sustain Christian ordinances in their efficiency. It must not be concealed, therefore, that, so far as the Memorial character of the object is concerned, there is still some hazard. For the present, the preservation of the design is rather dependent on individual firmness, than on public enthusiasm in England.

The extreme pressure on the pastor at one time existing is now removed. There are a " few noble " in the old country who are ready to coöperate.

To our regret, the Ex-Lord Mayor of London is prevented from taking part in the work by severe and protracted indisposition. The Chamberlain of the city of London is our friend. Mr. Apsley Pellatt has rendered valuable service with Mr. John Olney, — and no one has evinced a more constant and steady regard for the interests of the church, than Mr. W. Armitage of Manchester.

There is ground, therefore, for encouragement and for renewed effort. It would gratify my own feelings much to inscribe here the names of our friends in America, but the list is with Mr. James Lawrence of Boston and Mr. W. G. Lambert of New York. Let us try again, — and if we live to see the completion of the Memorial building in Southwark, I will prepare a sketch of the history of the church, giving, in an appendix, the names of those who have taken part in its erection.

J. W.

4 SURREY SQUARE, OLD KENT ROAD,
LONDON, May 16, 1860.

CONTENTS.

		PAGE
INTRODUCTION,	. . . .	xi
I.	CONFORMITY AND ITS ENFORCEMENT, . . .	1
II.	THE SEPARATIST FIRST PRINTER, . . .	26
III.	THE PURITANS AND SEPARATISTS, . . .	45
IV.	SEPARATIST PRINCIPLES FROM THE PRISONS, . .	51
V.	ELECTION OF CHURCH OFFICERS, ...	70
VI.	ARRESTED CHURCH MEMBERS. — BARROWE'S LETTERS,	75
VII.	PENRY, THE PILGRIM MARTYR, . .	98
VIII.	FIRST PLANS FOR MIGRATING TO NEW ENGLAND, .	109
IX.	MORE IMPRISONMENTS. — FRANCIS JOHNSON, .	116
X.	THE SECOND SEPARATION. — BREWSTER AND THE CHURCH AT SCROOBY MANOR, . . .	133
XI.	PERSECUTIONS. — MRS. CHURCHMAN, . . .	147
XII.	DIFFICULTIES IN REACHING HOLLAND, . . .	155
XIII.	PILGRIM LIFE IN AMSTERDAM, . . .	160
XIV.	THE PILGRIM PASTOR IN LEYDEN, . . .	166

CONTENTS.

XV.	SECOND PILGRIM CHURCH. — HENRY JACOB, .	179
XVI.	DISCUSSIONS ON LEAVING HOLLAND, . . .	193
XVII.	NEGOTIATIONS AND CONCLUSIONS CONCERNING VIRGINIA, ...	201
XVIII.	BREWER AND BREWSTER THE BROWNIST PRINTERS,	210
XIX.	CUSHMAN'S NEGOTIATIONS. — THE MAYFLOWER,	228
XX.	THE DEBARKATION FROM LEYDEN, . . .	240
XXI.	THE VOYAGE AND THE LANDING, . .	251
INDEX, ...		301

INTRODUCTION.

The declaration of independence by the North American Congress was an act purely political. It had more reference to the stolid British administration than to the noble race from which we sprang. Accordingly, from the day the government of the two countries had become two, the people have been becoming more thoroughly one. And this union, strengthened by very various influences, has now become so firm, that neither the war of 1812, nor the base cupidity of British merchants and ship-builders, nor the intrigues of a republic-hating, slavery-loving aristocracy in 1863, can destroy it.

Whatever course the present generation of Britons may pursue, the old British heir-loom, the old British history, will still be ours. We have never lost our rights in the ancient family possessions. And, if the day should ever arrive when the people of this country lose their interest in that history, it will be a day of degeneracy, and not of progress.

We are mainly Britons in origin. In the character, the language, the religion, the literature, and the characteristic institutions of our country, it is neither the Indian, the Gaul, the German, nor the Hollander, whose impress we behold. Our whole political, literary, social, and religious history finds its origin and its type in British history and character.

To what section, then, of British history, and to what class of the English race, does the Republic of North America owe most of its peculiar character and its distinguishing political and religious institutions? We reply without hesitation; to the men who, under the Tudors and Stuarts, separated themselves most fully from the church established by law in Great Britain. And it is equally evident that our indebtedness becomes the more complete the further we advance from the class of simple Protestants within that church, up through the partially reformed Puritan ranks, to the Independents, who most profoundly examined the whole subject of church government, and the relations of the church to the State. The principles that for more than eighty years have been applied to human society on this vast continent, from the lakes to the gulf, from the Atlantic to the Pacific, by thirty millions of people, were mainly wrought out by a little, despised band in England, three hundred years ago. And yet, strenuous efforts have recently been made to diminish our interest in these men, to deny to them the glory of having introduced into our national character some of its best qualities.

It has been affirmed, also, that there is room for serious doubt "whether the colonization of any portion of our land originated in religious persecution; or, chiefly in schemes for the pursuit of gain, with the desire of the undisputed right to maintain peculiar religious dogmas and politics, without any contradiction." It has been said, that "the Pilgrim Fathers thought only of liberty for themselves, not for humanity," and that, "but for Roger Williams, this Union never could have existed to the present day."* It has been said that they left us an example of much that should be shunned.

Even were it the case that all these affirmations represented the reality of things, our interest in British history, and especially in the history of "Dissent," would still be very great.

This nation's roots were planted at Jamestown, New Amsterdam, and Plymouth. Only three of the many colonies established within the limits of the present United States were permanent and influential. But when we contrast the training of the Pilgrims with that of the Cavaliers, or of the Dutch adventurers; when we contrast their purposes in coming to these shores; the respective organization of each company; the characters of the men; their antecedent history; their course here; and their actual influence, — there remains no room to doubt that the character of this Republic owes more to the Pilgrims of Leyden and Plymouth than to any others of our ancestors.

What does history know of the colonists of Jamestown or New Amsterdam, as a body, before their settlement here? Nay, what did they know of each other?

---

* Newspaper report of Dr. Wayland's Speech on Roger Williams.

B

The Plymouth colony was a unit. It was a living organism, born from heaven, nurtured in the sternest school of suffering, led by the God of Israel through a desert, out of the house of bondage, into this its promised land. The Pilgrims were men raised up for a peculiar and a great end, and peculiarly trained for it by that mighty hand which always shapes its own instruments, and tempers its best in the hottest fires.

The Pilgrims were students of the best writings of antiquity. They culled from all the treasures of literature the principles most serviceable to human society, that they might embody them in living institutions.

They accepted the doctrine that governments were made for the people; and in this wilderness they established the principle that the majority must govern in all common interests, civil or ecclesiastical. They believed that the education of the laborer was the duty of society. They founded a society which recognized the legal equality of all men. They established the principle that only regenerated men ought to enter the church and its ministry, and that credible evidence of a new heart should be required of all applying for admission to either.

It is not claimed for them that they were never anticipated in any of these views. All here affirmed is, that some of the most important ecclesiastical principles were discovered by themselves; that they first incorporated others before discovered, and at immense sacrifice, into living institutions; and that their predecessors in thought or action were the noblest specimens of the race.

It was their peculiarity to have recognized that the

church had in their day reached its maturity, and was no longer to be held "under tutors and governors." They denied not the good there once was in Judaism, Romanism, Prelacy, and Semi-prelacy. But all that was good and peculiar in them was adapted to the state of pupilage in the church. It was equally so with human society; at least, English society, in regard to monarchy, feudal sovereignty, and aristocratic institutions. These they set aside, as a man full-grown puts away childish things. They, in a word, only carried out the Reformation some steps further than the German and French reformers.

Could the writer, we have quoted, have been serious when he expressed a doubt whether Brewster and Carver really came to this new world as commercial adventurers, or as religious exiles seeking a sanctuary for the pure worship of God?

Is it not possible for these men of God to find rest, even in their graves, from such injustice? If we had no other testimony than that furnished by their own writings, prepared under circumstances which preclude the admissibleness of the idea that they had any supreme reference to colonizing a country, establishing a civil government, or making an increase of their worldly wealth, we should reject this theory. With their own writings in our hand we must believe that the secession from the church of England, and the voluntary expatriation of the men who founded the colony of Plymouth, were as purely conscientious and religious a series of acts as ever men performed.

And while we cheerfully recognize in the Huguenots, the Scotch, and the Dutch colonies, in many of the Cavaliers, and even in Pocahontas, a lofty type of character; and while we acknowledge how much this country owes of her position and possessions to them; while we delight to recall the actions of men like Nathaniel Bacon and others, noble Virginians, who overthrew the tyranny of Berkley, and who wrought out the freedom of the colonies in part, even a century before it was matured, yet we must believe that all the higher interests of society, the departments of education, theology, commerce, manufactures, have been more thoroughly advanced by New England and her migrating sons, than by any other section of the nation.

This is the only country whose origin and history embody these great principles: the will of the majority shall be expressed in the choice of civil rulers; the rights of the people shall be guarded by a constitution; and man shall exercise his own convictions and judgment in matters of religion. These principles we express by the terms, — civil freedom, liberty of conscience.

There are, indeed, those among us who, in view of the extravagant lengths to which the democratical principle is urged by many, are now entertaining doubts whether the establishment of these principles, and their incorporation into the institutions of society was a real progress of the human race. And when the example of these States was recently employed to secure the success of certain political measures in Great Britain, eminent statesmen declared unqualifiedly that our grand experiment is a failure. And even so liberal a political philosopher as Lord Macaulay has left his testimony very much to the same effect.

Should the result of all this discussion and this discouraging estimate of our prospects be, to induce in our people more serious inquiries into the peculiar principles of our social system, and into the history of that terrible conflict through which their discoverers and defenders were compelled to pass, they will be to the cause of humanity a great benefit.

This is not the place for the discussion of political principles, and yet we cannot refrain from referring to the peculiar character of the war now raging in our beloved land. What are the avowed principles and aims of its originators? Their principles are those of Feudalism and Chivalry; their aim is to crush Puritanism, to thrust Massachusetts out of the Union, and secure an oligarchical government. Why is their animosity directed to Massachusetts particularly; why to New England generally; why is "Yankee" the chosen epithet to inflame the animosity of their people? All indicates that they feel the working of the old Puritan leaven, just as Laud and Jeffries felt it in former days. Let us, then, distinctly state the question between the two parties, in a form which, to many minds, is itself a decision of the point at issue. The question, then, is simply this: If men are not competent to govern themselves, are they competent to govern other people? If not, is a human government possible? It will, indeed, be said, the capacity for government is as rare an endowment as any other peculiar talent, being confined to the few. If we grant that position, then the question arises, What is the most desirable method of discovering who possesses both the genius for ruling, and the probity that will secure its right exercise? We say there cannot be any infallible method. And of the two, popular election and hereditary succession, we prefer the former from our knowledge of the past and of men. And we should cite Great Britain itself in proof of the correctness of our position, because many of her hereditary rulers have been the most incompetent in the nation; and her house of commons, which is her real ruler, is elective.

But our interest in the work here introduced arises not so much from its relations to our political history, as from its connection with the gospel of Christ and liberty of conscience.

It has been said that the Pilgrims sought liberty only for themselves. Well, this is confessedly a great deal. Wallace was not seeking liberty for mankind, nor Tell, nor the heroes of Marathon. Yet the world has canonized them. Why not the poor pilgrims then? There are two kinds of heroes. The one class seek liberty for the whole race. They sit in snug libraries, and write heroic stanzas about universal liberty. There are others who try, at every sacrifice of inferior interests, both to maintain the true doctrine of human rights, and to gain their own freedom. The Pilgrims were of this class.

In regard to the claims made in behalf of Roger Williams, if this were the place we should enter some qualifying protests. But, admit them all; it then remains true that he was an Englishman, a Puritan, a Pilgrim; that while he did comprehend more clearly than his brethren the nature and extent of the rights of the individual conscience, he did not comprehend as fully as they the rights of associated consciences. He claimed not only the right of thinking for himself, but also of disturbing others in the enjoyment of their rights. The universal adoption of his views and practices would have made the existence of government an impossibility. We accept the judgment of him which Professor Stowe * has pronounced. He "was an honest, good man; at heart a Christian. The great duty of religious toleration he saw clearly, and practised consistently. In this he was greatly in advance of most men of his age." Yet "no commonwealth, especially in times of feebleness and danger, could, without self-annihilation, tolerate such a course as he sometimes took in regard to the government of the colonies." We have surely seen much to illustrate this in the course taken by many citizens of the free States during this rebellion. Self-preservation demanded their ejection from a country whose hands they were weakening in the day of its trial.

But we have heard still other charges.

The Pilgrims have been called "schismatics, fanatics, and persecutors."

What is a schism? Etymologically, Abraham was a schismatic; so were the apostles; so was the church of England. All of these separated from the church of their fathers and their nation. Every separation, then,

* Bib. Sacra, VII. 106.

is not schismatic. That quality is determined by the circumstances and motives of the separation. Had, then, the Independents sufficient reason for changing their ecclesiastical position?

That great religious movement, emphatically called the Reformation, was probably nowhere so incomplete in its origin, character, and immediate results as within the pale of the Anglican church! In no other nation was it so prominently a political movement in its original aims, spirit, and measures, as in England. There were, undoubtedly, men among the English reformers as godly, as learned, as evangelical, as Luther, Calvin, Knox, or Zuingle. But, while in every other country the revolution was achieved by clergymen mainly, in England the royal will was its mainspring, and the royal hand its guide.

Two sterner wills never swayed the sceptre of dominion than those of Henry VIII. and Elizabeth, the father and the foster-mother of the English Reformation. That either of them knew the gospel experimentally, we find ourselves unable to believe; and we regard it not uncharitable to say it, while examining the history of the Protestant Episcopal Church. For all that is godly in its ministry and its members we are devoutly thankful to Him from whom all good descends. But when our brethren claim some historical preëminence above those who build with them upon Christ, the only foundation, we must put in our protest. We would, indeed, hold no individual in our day responsible for the tyranny and cruelty of Laud and Whitgift. But we maintain, that when a branch of the church claims a historical superiority to other branches, it must, in honesty, take the whole of their peculiar history. This is the mill-stone around the neck of the Roman church. So far as we exult in being of the Pilgrim church, we must take that church in its individual and entire history. If its origin had been in lust, and pride, and covetousness, then we should feel constrained to say, not "our glorious apostolical church," but, "a Syrian was our father," and we will henceforth glory not in what distinguishes us from men who may be as pleasing to God as ourselves, but in Christ, who belongs equally to all believers.

English history is a solemn illustration of that process of judgment which is advancing to its culminating scene at the end of our world's probation. How long had we been accustomed to the servile representations of Hume and the court historians! What name has been more blackened than that of Oliver Cromwell! For more than two centuries the name of Browne, a renegade, has been thrown as mud, at the images of the Pilgrims; and Penry has been synonymous with the vilest names in the English vocabulary. But slowly and surely the truth is coming to light; and men's moral judgments are undergoing great changes. If nothing else, the prominent influence of the Pilgrims, in forming the character of this republic, has called for a new investigation into their history. Surely Robinson and Brewster and Barrowe and Johnson and Greenwood could not have been such men as history has been accustomed to depict them, and yet have moulded such a nation as this, to such an extent, by their writings and spirit.

Another historian now invites us to open some new chapters of the martyr-history and the martyr-literature of our fatherland. From their own and contemporaneous writings, from those most affecting records, found on the scraps of paper obtained in prison without the consent of my lord the archbishop, and moistened with the tears of men now in heaven, to whose story angels have probably listened with admiration, we have here an opportunity of forming, on authoritative grounds, our estimate of the character and aims of the men prominent in ultimately giving to the English Reformation its completeness and its true development.

None of our ancestors have laid us under such a debt as those who purchased our freedom by suffering long imprisonments; our wealth, by their own deep poverty; our joys, by their own sorrows; and it is due to ourselves as well as them, that we should rid our minds of all prejudices and false apprehensions in regard to them.

The exiles of Leyden were called Brownists, but most unjustly. Browne was a renegade who advocated their principles for a time, and then betrayed them. They were denominated Schismatic: but the epithet is ambiguous. To rend one's self from a corrupt church, is to follow the apostles and the whole primitive church. Episcopalian and Independent of this day are alike indebted to these men for their protests, so intelligently and meekly made, so firmly maintained, even to martyrdom. They were accused by their enemies of austerity. It has been well said of Knox, that he "had been charged with barbarism, and, truly or untruly represented as saying, that the rookeries of cathedrals must fall, or the rooks of the clergy would return." But the Papacy did that, and worse than that, in the case of the Port-Royalists. "It swept out the doves, and hewed down the dovecote that the owl might sleep in peace, and the raven not be shamed by comparison with the birds of a sweeter voice and brighter wing." If they were austere, what else could they be toward such evils as they were called upon to resist! So were the Lord and his apostles austere. The real question is, Were they too indignant at the wickedness in the high places of the church? But the reader of this compilation will be led to observe that there were very distinct classes of men protesting against the evils of the Anglican church. Those to whom New England traces her origin, were of two classes, — the Puritans, who remained in the Established church after discovering its errors, and the Independents, who emigrated to the continent. Some of their leaders were men who were ranked among the first scholars of England. In that whole body of believers to which such men as Robinson and Greenwood ministered, we can see no signs of a fierce, sour, splenetic spirit. Let the reader pause when he sees the pastors in prison examining members for admission to their persecuted church, marking them as it were for the slaughter. Let him read Penry's letters to his wife, from the midst of a loathsome prison, surrounded by men more loathsome still; let him read Barrowe's petition to the queen; and then, while he witnesses the outpourings of a husband's love, of a father's pity for his helpless children; as he witnesses the throbbings of hearts full of meekness, tenderness, loyalty, patriotism, and Christian courage, then, while the tears obscure his vision of the page, let him ponder the question, Are these the austere, sour fanatics of whom so much has been said?

The Puritans may have persecuted when their chance came ; but just the difference between them and the Pilgrims was, that the former studied the questions of doctrine and church polity superficially, and the latter profoundly. The Puritans had half learned their lesson ; the Pilgrims learned it all. They were not persecutors when in England or New England ; and when we are severe upon the Puritans, we should remember that in their day Charles and Laud governed by will, not by a constitution. We must remember that even Elizabeth suffered such wretches as Matthew of Canterbury to fine, imprison, mutilate, and murder Englishmen at their pleasure. We can never excuse persecution or retaliation ; but men need not have been much worse than the most of us, to have done something of the kind when they lived in an age in which, by the will of one or a few, judges were displaced, municipal charters suspended, the press silenced, taxes levied, parliament not convened for long periods, but the Star Chamber in constant session and active operation!

These men have been denominated "Fanatics." But this we understand merely to mean, they believed the Scriptures really to be the word of God ; heaven, hell, prayer, repentance, holiness, salvation, to be realities ; solemn, immortal realities in themselves or in their relations.

Let the question be proposed, and fairly answered: What has been the character and results of their influence in the world?

They discovered or applied some of the most important principles in religion and government, which had never before been theoretically so stated and practically so applied. Some of those principles are now so familiar to us, that it may be difficult to realize it ever required an extraordinary independence, energy, and courage to discover, avow, or apply them. Take, for example, the right and duty of exercising personal judgment in ascertaining the truth, and you have before you a principle, the opposite of which is, an absurdity to our minds. And yet this was the sum and substance of the heresy, fanaticism, impiety, and treason for which our godly predecessors were hunted as wild beasts, and destroyed as vermin.

In their melancholy history the English mind discovered fully that, however desirable it may be that all men should think alike, and think aright on religious subjects, yet such uniformity can never be the result of coercion or political measures. When the human race shall have become wholly orthodox, it will first have been wholly free from the constraint of human authority, civil or ecclesiastical.

Some historians have discovered, and avowed that Britain mainly owes the chief elements of her greatness to her Calvinists and her Dissenters. If we should concede to the learned and lamented Sir J. Stephen, that "England owes her greatness to her noble and sacerdotal classes, who have secured the growth and maintenance of her constitutional liberties," yet we should insist that there were periods when it was by martyr-patience and the might of meekness, endurance, and toil, that those liberties were wrung from the reluctant grasp of the hierarchy by men and women who belong neither to the noble orders nor to the State hierarchy.

The glory of the Puritans and Pilgrims is, not so much that they gave the world the religious and civil institutions out of which this republic sprang, but that they reformed, or, rather, completed the Reformation. They brought religion back to its vital principles; they showed it to be a personal union with Christ by a personal faith, which neither churches, nor functionaries, nor ceremonies can impart nor destroy, but to which it is their highest glory to minister, even in the obscurest believer.

It is time the history of these men were better known than they generally are; their characters seen apart from oddities of costumes, of names, and of manners; their religious faith seen to be the source of their noble deeds and institutions; and their example recognized as a light on the pathway of humanity.

The tendency of human nature is, to work backward from a heroic age and race to unheroic principles and customs. A few thinkers, at least, in every generation, ought to have those principles fresh in their memory. The discussions and researches by which reformers have reached their conclusions, ought to be so familiar to at least a few leading minds, that society need not be forever moving in a circle, and returning upon its own track.

But, patient reader, it is time you should be introduced to our author. He, and his works, will not need a second introduction to the people of this continent. Having a mind capable of distinguishing, and a heart capable of appreciating those grand elements of character so prominent in that struggle for spiritual emancipation, and in that defence of spiritual religion which resulted in giving America her richest treasure, he is peculiarly fitted for making these researches. But we will not gratify our own feelings at the expense of his, whose modesty and simplicity of character would but be offended at any thing that should obtrude him between this book and its reader. If, however, we may not thus commend him to the reader's confidence, we may speak of his peculiar qualification for the task here undertaken, in the possession of so many genuine documents, such a mine of Puritan literature, heretofore unedited, unknown, safe from the unwise meddling of friendly emendation, and beneath the notice of unfriendly eyes. Let us admire the ways of Him who maketh "the wrath of man to praise him," while the remainder he will restrain. The churchman of Laud's day so hated the Independent follower of Christ, and so dreaded the influence of his writings, that, while he was burned or exiled, his manuscripts, letters, diaries, narratives, petitions, and remonstrances, his papers were taken from him. But why were they not burned? Ashes preach no heresy. Aye, indeed! why were they not destroyed? The wrath of man would naturally have done that. But that wrath was restrained, and the enemies of the Puritans and Pilgrims, the men who intended to prevent the spreading of their principles, were merely used by Providence to deposit these sacred seeds in a safe place, that they might be brought out in due time, to be scattered in a soil ready to receive them.

And what more opportune than this effort to sow them in the hearts of this people, when these very principles are working their way, as we trust, to victory, through strife and bloodshed! The Cavalier and the Roundhead seem now met for the last time, to determine which shall have this broad field for sowing his seed; which set of principles shall mould the coming millions on this continent. God speed the right!

TRACK OF THE HIDDEN CHURCH.

I.

THE inquiry, on which we propose to enter, is not unlike a descent into the catacombs. The explorer of the subterranean region which contains the memorials of Christian confessors, leaves, for a time, the breathing world, to enter alone, and with a feeble light, hidden recesses, long forgotten, and almost unknown. The silence is oppressive. He is startled, at first, by the sound of his own footsteps; but, as he gains confidence, the sense of strangeness and of solitude is lost in the interest he feels in deciphering the inscriptions which remain upon the broken fragments around him; to tell in their touching and eloquent simplicity of the conflicts and sufferings of the faithful, — whose names, once cast out as evil, are now brought to grateful and instructive remembrance.

Our aim is to trace the course of men of whom the world was not worthy, and who have no place in its history. The memorial of them would have perished, if those who took their lives had not also seized their books and papers. These precious documents remain in the care of Providence, undisturbed, from the circumstance that for nearly three centuries they were accessible only to those who had no curiosity to look into them.

Here, for example, are prison letters written in haste, and with many tears; petitions for relief, to which the distressed suppliants durst not append their signatures; broken and hurried communications from stern oppressors, vexed with the constancy they could not subdue, and irritated by the failure of all their plans to silence the humble witnesses for truth whom they affected to despise.

From these and similar fragmentary memorials, we are to make out the story of the Hidden Church.

We confess, at the outset, that we are at serious disadvantage from the want of an appropriate designation. The names given to the early pioneers of truth and freedom in England were intended only as terms of reproach. They do not, therefore, give a fair representation of their principles. We shall have to speak of them as Separatists and Brownists; but they might rather be called the Nazarenes of the Reformation. Like their Master, they were hated and opposed by all parties, because of the truth to which they were called to bear witness. To determine their relative position, and to mark their progress, it will be useful to glance at the facts of contemporaneous history.

The accession of Elizabeth to the throne of England was the signal for the return of the exiles who had fled to the continent in the Marian persecution. They hastened to their native land in the expectation of seeing the principles of the Reformation fully carried out. But in this hope they were destined to suffer severe disappointment. They soon found that the form of the new establishment was to be determined rather by the requirements of a comprehensive state policy, than by a direct appeal to Scripture. The queen assumed absolute supremacy in ecclesiastical matters; and it was her aim, by an ingenious compromise, at once to reconcile the Romanist and to accommodate the Protestant within the pale of the church to be called into existence in obedience to her royal pleasure. She insisted that there should be an immediate truce from religious controversy, and that all parties should yield, in things spiritual as well as temporal, unqualified submission to her sole authority.

With some reluctance, a section of the Anglican reformers acquiesced in the system proposed for their adoption. They would have preferred a system of church polity more consistent with their personal views, but they feared lest the power and emoluments of the episcopate should revert to the secret adherents of the papacy. They yielded to expediency, and overcame their scruples, to enjoy the temporal advantages of which they had for a long time been deprived. A few of their number, to the credit of their profession, declined to accept office at the expense of sincerity. Notwithstanding the gilded bait, they held their faith with a good conscience. As they found opportunity, they continued to instruct the people in places remote from the observation of the court, and in the quietest manner, to avoid offence. In the letters exchanged between the reformers in England and their brethren on the continent, we learn the state of things, and the various mental conflicts to which it naturally gave rise. "I had once," says one of them, "a little cottage at Zurich, and if God would grant my wishes, I should most anxiously return to it." He felt as a stranger in the land of his birth, and sighed for the congenial society and the simple ordinances of Christian worship he had enjoyed on the banks of the peaceful lake in a Swiss canton. The experience of Thomas Lever is illustrative, though he was more favored than many of his brethren. In a letter to Bullinger, dated Coventry, July 10, 1560, he writes: "No discipline is as yet established by any public authority. Many of our parishes have no clergymen, and some dioceses are without a bishop; and out of that small number who administer the sacrament throughout this great country, there is hardly one in a hundred who is both able and willing to preach the word of God; but all persons are obliged to read only what is prescribed in the books.

"If you wish for any tidings respecting myself, I would have you know that immediately after my return to England, I travelled through a great part of it for the sake of preaching the gospel; and there is a city in the middle of England called Coventry, in which there have always been, since the revival of the gospel, great numbers zealous for evangelical truth; so that in the last persecution under Mary, some were burned (at the stake), and others went into banishment with myself; and the remainder, long tossed about in great difficulty and distress, have at last, on the restoration of pure religion, invited other preachers, and myself in particular, to proclaim the gospel to them at Coventry. After I had discovered, by the experience of some weeks, that vast numbers in this place were in the habit of frequenting public preaching of the gospel, I consented to their request, that I should settle my wife and family among them; and thus, now for nearly a whole year, I have preached to them without any hinderance, and they have liberally maintained me and my family in this city. For we are not bound to each other, neither to the townsmen, nor they to me, by any law or engagement, but only by free kindness and love." The best of bonds surely in such relations.

These services in Coventry, however, were exceptional, and held only on sufferance. Stringent measures were soon adopted to reduce all ministers and congregations to the same ecclesiastical order, and it was determined to allow no variation in the mode of worship. Subscription was required to the thirty-nine articles in 1562, and orders were issued in 1564 for the suppression of preaching, except by the clergy who should engage on oath to comply with every part of the regulations with respect to ceremonies. Earnest remonstrances were uttered by divines of the soundest learning, and of the most exemplary piety. "I understand," said William Whittingham, "they are about to compel us, contrary to our consciences, to wear the popish apparel, or deprive us of our ministry and livings. Yet when I consider the weighty charge enjoined upon us by the Almighty God, and the exact account we have to give of the right use and faithful dispensation of His mysteries, I cannot doubt which to choose. . . . What agreement can the superstitious inventions have with the pure word of God? What edification can there be when the Spirit of God is grieved, the children of God discouraged, wicked papists confirmed, and a door opened for such popish traditions and wicked impiety? Can that be called true liberty, where a yoke is laid on the necks of the disciples; where the conscience is clogged with impositions; where faithful preachers are threatened with deprivation; where congregations are robbed of the learned and godly pastors; and where the holy sacraments are made subject to superstitious and idolatrous vestments? ... If we compel the servants of Christ to conform unto the papists, I greatly fear we shall return again to popery."

"Our case, my Lord, will be deplorable, if such compulsion should be used against us, while so much lenity is used toward the papists. How many papists enjoy their liberty and livings, who have neither sworn obedience to the queen's majesty, nor discharged their duty to their miserable flocks! These men laugh and triumph to see us treated thus, and are not ashamed of boasting, that they hope the rest of popery will soon return. My Lord, pity the disconsolate churches. Hear the cries and groans of many thousands of God's poor children, hungering and thirsting after spiritual food. I need not appeal to the word of God, to the history of the primitive church, to the just judgments of God poured out upon the nations for lack of true reformation. Judge ye betwixt us and our enemies

And if we seek the glory of God alone, the enjoyment of true Christian liberty, the overthrow of all idolatry and superstition, and to win souls to Christ; I beseech your honor to pity our case, and to use your utmost endeavors to secure unto us our liberty."

Insensible to such appeals, and regardless of the churches deprived of their preachers, the prelates enforced the rule of uniformity with greater rigor.

Archbishop Parker and Bishop Grindal, in a joint communication to Secretary Cecil, dated "Lambeth, the 20th of March, 1565," express their determination to bring the clergy to submission: "We mean to call all manner of pastors and curates within the city of London to appear before us at Lambeth in the Chapel there, and to expound the cause, and say some things to move them to conformity, with intimations of the penalty which necessarily must ensue against the recusants. After the general exposition, as aforesaid, to the whole number, we intend particularly to examine every one of them, whether they will promise conformity in their ministrations and outward apparel established by law and injunction, and testify the same by subscription at their hands. It is intended presently to suspend all such as refuse to promise conformity in the premises; and also to pronounce sequestration of their ecclesiastical livings, from and after the day of our Lady next, being now at hand. And after such sequestrations, if they be not reconciled within three months, to proceed to deprivation of their livings by due form of law. We may make an intimation of the sarcenet tippet, to such as may wear it by act of parliament, Anno Hen. VIII., and as to move them, if this be thought good. In fine, we think very many of the churches will be destitute of their pastors; and that many will forsake their livings, and live at printing, teaching children, or otherwise as they can. That no tumult may follow what speeches and talks be likely to rise in the realm, and presently in the whole city by this, we leave it to your wisdom to confer; and we trust that the Queen's Majesty will send some honorable to join with us two, to authorize the rather her commandment and pleasure, as your honor signified unto me was proposed. And thus praying your honor to consult with whom your wisdom shall think most meet, that we may be resolved, and that on Friday, the parties summoned for their appearance on Saturday following, at one of the clock, order may be taken, or else after these two holidays, on Tuesday afternoon at the farthest."*

The calculation of forces seems to have been carefully made by the two episcopal commanders.

---

* Lansdowne MSS., Vol. 8, No. 86.

A "general exposition," followed by a little persuasion, with intimations of the penal consequences of non-compliance. The reserved force they looked for to the secular authorities. The coolness with which these chief pastors anticipated the privation and distress that would ensue to the conscientious clergy is characteristic.

No time was lost. The Chapel at Lambeth was filled on the 26th of the same month with the pastors and curates of the metropolis summoned for the occasion. Apparently to give dramatic effect to the proceedings, Mr. Robert Cole, just enriched with two benefices in London, presented himself in the priestly habits according to the authorized pattern, not excepting the "sarcenet" tippet. "My masters," cried the bishop chancellor, as he pointed to the *tableau vivant*, "and ye ministers of London, the Council's pleasure is, that strictly ye keep the unity of apparel, like this man who stands here canonically habited with a square cap, a scholar's gown, priest-like, and, in the church, a linen surplice. Ye that will subscribe, write *volo;* those that will not subscribe, write *nolo*. Make no words."

Some of the ministers attempted to speak. "Peace! Peace!" cried the Chancellor. "Apparitor! call over the churches. Ye masters, answer presently under the penalty of contempt."

John Fox, the venerable martyrologist, was first

called. Taking his Greek Testament out of his pocket, he said: "To this will I subscribe. I have nothing in the church but a prebend in Salisbury, and much good may it do you, if you take it from me."

The majority succumbed; but notwithstanding the pressure upon them, many had courage to say "Nolo." Some of them had been companions in exile for the faith, and to preserve a good conscience they were ready to suffer the loss of all things.

The victory of the prelates, therefore, was only partial. The subscribers had the greatest cause for humiliation. "We are killed," they said, "in our souls by this pollution. We cannot perform our ministry in the singleness of our hearts." The Archbishop hastened to report the result of the proceedings. His letter to Cecil conveys his impressions at the time:

"SIR, — I must signify to your honors what this day we have done in the examination of the London ministers. Sixty-one promised conformity. Nine or ten were absent. Thirty-seven denied; of which number were the best, and some preachers; six or seven are diligent, sober men, pretending conscience. Divers of them zealous, but of little learning. We did suspend them, and sequestered the fruits, and from all manner of ministry, with signification, that if they would not reconcile themselves within three months, then to be deprived. They showed reasonable quietness and modesty, otherwise than I looked for. I think some of them must come in, when they shall feel their want; especially such as but in a spiced fancy held out. Some of them were moved in a conference, wherein I labored by some advertisements to pacify; but they would not grieve. It is not felt as, I think, it will be hereafter. Some of them alleged that there were fruits, and would have some toleration, or discharge of payment. I answered, I could not so dispense, and left them to their fate.

Thus your honor hath all worth the writing. I pray your honor to move my Lord of London to execute the order. My Lord of Ely did write me a letter, wherein he did signify, that if London were reformed, all the realm would soon follow, as I believe the same. This 26th of March, 1566."

" Your honor's, always in Christ,"

" MATTHEW CANT."

It must be admitted that " Matthew Cant." pressed the siege with uncommon vigor. To starve the " Nolos " into surrender the sooner, he resolved to exact the dividends in the shape of " fruits," even when the income of the poor incumbent was sequestered.

But we turn aside from the semi-political and semi-religious contest connected with the question of vestments so often described in puritan history, to mark the course of the moral conflict entered into by men of another order. There were Christian people in London at this time who had stood their ground in the midst of all the Marian troubles. When the leaders of the reformation in England were driven into exile or burnt at the stake, these humble Christian confessors continued to meet for worship. Not a few of their brethren passed through the ordeal of martyrdom. The simple notices of them to be found in the "acts and monuments," evince their spirit. The pastor, John Rough, tells us (September 17, 1557) that he attended the burning of four martyrs at Islington "to learn the way." On the 27th of June, 1566, twenty thousand persons stood around the blazing faggots which consumed thirteen brethren at Bow. The object of their coming to that appalling scene was "to strengthen themselves in the profession of the gospel, and to exhort and to comfort those who were to die." Bentham went with his congregation to Smithfield, on the 28th of June, 1558, to witness the burning of Holland and six of his companions. Standing before the assembled multitude, and in defiance of the prohibitory law, the intrepid pastor, in a loud voice, said: " Almighty God, for Christ's sake, help them." All the people gave the response, "Amen! Amen!"

The decrees of Lambeth only stimulated such men to reiterate their good confession. It is true that, to the proud and intolerant hierarchy, their movements appeared to be almost ridiculous, except for its annoyance. Bishop Grindal, speaking of them to Bullinger, says: "Some London citizens of the lowest order, together with four or five ministers, remarkable neither for judgment nor learning, have openly separated from us, and sometimes in private houses, sometimes in the fields, and occasionally even in ships, they have held their meetings and administer the sacraments. Besides this, they have ordained ministers and elders, after their own way." It is a consolation to his Lordship of London that the sect consists "of more women than men." There is a singular coincidence between the expressions of the prelate and those of Celsus, the first writer against Christianity. That infidel opponent jeeringly says: "Wool workers, cobblers, leather-dressers, the most illiterate and vulgar of mankind, were zealous preachers of the gospel, and addressed themselves, particularly in the outset, to women and children."

The halls belonging to the various city companies of London have, at different periods, afforded shelter and accommodation for persecuted Christians who desired to meet for worship. The congregation held in Plumbers' Hall which was surprised there June 16, 1567, does not seem, however, to have had the sanction of the civil authorities. The sheriffs of London broke upon them and found about one hundred persons present. Most of them were apprehended and taken to the compter. Next day Robert Hawkins, William White, Thomas Bowland, John Smith, William Nixon, James Ireland, and Richard Morecraft, were brought before Bishop Grindal, Dean Goodman, Archdeacon Watts, the Lord Mayor, and other commissioners. The Bishop charged them with absenting themselves from the parish churches, and with setting up separate assemblies for prayer, preaching, and administering the sacrament. The inquisitorial examination to which they were subjected, has often been printed, so that we have no need to reproduce it here; but it is important to observe the names, because we shall find in them a link of connection with the church, of which original documents have very recently come to light. The appeal of the accused was to the Scripture. "We will be judged," they said, "by the word of God, which shall judge us all at the last day, and is, therefore, sufficient to judge us now." It was no part of the business of the judicial bench to enter into a scriptural argument, but to exact an unreasoning submission; failing which, they committed the prisoners to Bridewell (a jail between Fleet Street and Blackfriars Bridge). For two years they were left in bonds, finding little sympathy even with the more advanced reformers.

In the month of April, 1569, we find that twenty-four of the brethren were discharged by an order of council, namely, — Robert Hawkins, John Smith, John Ropes, James Ireland, William Nixson, Walter Hinkesman, Thomas Bowland, George Waddy, William Turner, John Nash, James Adderton, Thomas Lidford, Richard Langton, Alexander Lacy, John Leonard, Robert Tod, Roger Hawksworth, Robert Sparrow, Richard King, Christopher Coleman, John Benson, John Bolton, Robert Gates, and William White, with seven women, whose names are not given.

The two years spent in jail only deepened the convictions of these faithful brethren; and, on the repeated avowal of their sentiments, they were re-committed to prison. From original documents, in the State Paper Office, we learn that a voluntary church was organized under the pastoral care of Richard Fitz, of which Thomas Bowland, one of the Bridewell confessors, was chosen deacon. The precious fragments, so long concealed, and now first printed, must excite a strong desire for further discoveries in relation to this deeply interesting witnessing community.

The following brief manifesto exhibits its character:

"*The True Marks of Christ's Church, etc.* — The order of the privy church in London, which by the malice of Satan is falsely slandered and evil spoken of: the minds of them that by the strength and working of the Almighty, our Lord Jesus Christ, have set their hands and hearts to the pure, unmingled, and sincere worship of God, according to His blessed and glorious word in all things, only abolishing and abhorring all traditions and inventions of man whatsoever, in the same religion and service of our Lord God: knowing this always that the true and afflicted church of our Lord and Saviour Jesus Christ either hath, or else evermore continually under the cross striveth for to have:

"First and foremost, the glorious word and Evangel preached not in bondage, but freely and purely.

"Secondly, to have the sacraments ministered purely, only altogether according to the institution and good word of the Lord Jesus, without any tradition or invention of man.

"And, last of all, to have, not the filthy canon law, but discipline only and altogether agreeable to the same heavenly and Almighty word of our Lord Jesus Christ.

"RICHARD FITZ, *Minister.*"

After the death of their pastor, in prison, the members of the church, in 1571, prepared and signed a document to the following effect:

"According to the saying of the Almighty our God, Matt. xviii. 20: 'Wherever two or three are gathered in my name, there am I;' so we, a poor congregation whom God hath separated from the churches of England, and from the mingled and false worship therein used; out of the which assemblies the Lord our only Saviour hath called us, and still calleth, saying, 'Come out from among them, and separate yourselves from them, and touch no unclean thing, then I will receive you, and I will be your God, and ye shall be my sons and daughters, saith the Lord.' 2 Cor. vi. 17, 18. So God giveth us strength at this day. We do serve the Lord every Sabbath day in houses, and on the fourth day in the week we meet, or come together weekly, to use prayer, and exercise discipline on them as deserve it, by the strength and sure warrant of the Lord our God's word, as in Matt. xviii. 15–18; 2 Cor. v."

"Some of the clergy," they add, "through their pomp and covetousness, have brought the gospel of our Saviour Jesus Christ into such slander and contempt, that men do think, for the most part, that the papists do use and hold a better religion than those which call themselves Christians, 'and are not, but do lie.' Rev. iii. 9. The Holy Ghost saith: 'I beheld another beast coming up out of the earth, which had two horns like the Lamb.' So this secret and disguised Antichrist, to wit, this canon law, of which the branches and their maintainers, though not so openly, have by long imprisonment pined and then killed the Lord's servants (as our minister, Richard Fitz, Thomas Bowland, deacon, one Partridge, and Giles Fowler), and besides them a great multitude. The very walls of the prison about this city, as the Gatehouse, Bridewell, the Counters, the King's Bench, and the Marshalsea, the White Lyon, would testify God's anger against this land for such injustice and subtle persecution. Signed — Henry Sparrowe, Jasper Woston, John Kyng, Martin Tilman, John Davy, Odye Lowne, Elizabeth Hill, Joane Mavericke, Margaret Weever, Abraham Fox, Mary Meyer, Eliz. Rumney, Anne Hall, James Anbyn, John Leonarde, George Hames, John Thomas, Jane Evance, Elizabeth Leonarde, Jane Ireland, Eliz. Clarke, Mary Race, Helen Stokes, Sara Cole, Constance Fox, Eliz. Balforth, Joane Abraham."

And this is all we know of this simple minded and earnest people who, almost unconsciously, commenced the struggle for principles which have leavened society for three centuries in England and America. A few words written in sorrow, but with an invincible faith, on a sheet of paper kept in the archives of Queen Victoria, contain the only record of them known to be in existence. We look upon them with an interest deeper than that of the traveller who has reached the undoubted source of some mighty river. Is it too much to say: "From this little fountain sprung all our freedom of religion?"

The examination of William White, more or less identified with the members of this Hidden Church, exhibits their heroic spirit.

On the 18th of January, 1573, he was brought before the Lord Chief Justice, the Master of the Rolls, the Master of Requests, the Dean of Westminster, the Sheriff of London, the Clerk of the Peace, Mr. Gerard. A few extracts from the colloquy that ensued between the Bench and the prisoner will sufficiently indicate its character.

Sheriff. Where is his wife?

White. She is at home.

Sheriff. Was she not summoned, bailiff?

White. Though she were warned, I hope I may answer for myself.

Lord Chief Justice. Who is this?

White. White, if it please your honor.

Lord Chief Justice. White! as black as the devil.

White. Not so, my Lord; one of God's children.

After the usual brow-beating for not coming to the parish church, the *Master of Requests* said:

"You do not obey the queen's laws."

"Nay," added the *Dean*, before the prisoner had time to reply: "you disobey God, for God commandeth you to obey your prince; therefore in disobeying her in these things, you disobey God."

White. I do not avoid these things of contempt, but of conscience. In all other things, I am an obedient subject.

Lord Chief Justice. The Queen's Majesty was overseen not to make thee of her council; to make laws and orders for religion.

White. Not so, my Lord. I am to obey laws warranted by God's word.

Lord Chief Justice. Do the queen's laws command any thing against God's word?

White. I do not say so, my Lord.

Lord Chief Justice. Yes, marry, you do; and there I will hold you.

White. Only God and his laws are absolutely perfect; all men and their laws may err.

Evidently chafed, his Lordship felt it needful for the sake of preserving his judicial dignity, to disclaim all passion in the case, at the same time reddening with excitement, and turning to the prisoner, he exclaimed, "I know thee not, saving by this occasion; thou art the wickedest, and most contemptuous person that has come before me, since I sat in this commission."

White. Not so, my Lord; my conscience doth witness otherwise.

Gerard. White, you were released, thinking you would be conformable, but you are worse than ever.

White. Not so, if it please you.

Lord Chief Justice. He would have no laws.

White. If there were no laws, I would live like a Christian, and do no wrong, though I received wrong.

Lord Chief Justice. Thou art a rebel.

White. Not so, my Lord, a true subject.

Lord Chief Justice. Yea, I swear by God, thou art a very rebel, for thou wouldest draw thy sword, and lift up thy hand against thy prince, if time served.

White. My Lord, I thank God my heart standeth right toward God and my prince; and God will not condemn, though your honor hath so judged.

Lord Chief Justice. Take him away.

The prisoner expressed a wish that he might be sent to some prison near his house, and where he should not have again to pay the fees as he had paid them in other prisons. But in the temper of the judge it was not likely that any relief would be granted. "Marry, shall you pay them," grunted out his Lordship.

"It will cost you twenty pounds," said the Master of Requests, "I warrant you before you come out."

"God's will be done," replied White, as the officers dragged him from the court.

The abominations of a London jail of that period can scarcely be imagined in modern times. The wives of the prisoners made incessant, but fruitless appeals, to the judges for their release. Their petitions contain affecting allusions to the intolerable miseries endured in the filthy dungeons. " Most humbly we beseech your honors for God's cause to hear us," so runs one of their memorials now before us, " the wives of these poor preachers that have lain almost these five months in Newgate, to the utter spoil and impoverishing both of themselves and of their poor wives and children. The cold weather approaching cannot but greatly hurt them."

The constancy with which, for the truth's sake, they could bear up amidst so many privations, and in sufferings so manifold and protracted, is marvellous. How far they were from yielding, we may judge from a letter of White to Edward Deering, a Puritan minister. The rumor having reached him in prison, that this eminent divine was tempted to conceal the truth, or to modify his testimony, he could not refrain from offering words of fraternal admonition. We quote the following passages: " The grace of our Lord Jesus Christ be with you forever. Beloved Mr. Deering in the Lord Jesus. Forasmuch as it is reported that some would have you, with others, to qualify your doctrine from particular naming of those corruptions and maintainers thereof, which at this day are urged and used in this Church of England, I, being a simple brother, yet wishing sincerity in religion, with a thorough reformation (not doubting but you and your great wisdom, learning, and deep understanding in the Scriptures of God, through abundance of His spirit, are able to avoid the subtle sleights of Satan in his instruments, of which I fear the above named is one), I thought it my duty in the Lord to admonish you to take heed how you yield thereunto."

"Since neither the prophets, Christ, his apostles, nor any true preachers, through entreaty, flattery, or tyranny, were led to cease from preaching, or to frame their doctrines according to their fancy, therefore my hope is, you will not; but boldly, after the example of all the godly, as you have begun, go forward plainly and simply in the truth of God's gospel, which I, with my brethren, so earnestly desire of you, and most earnestly pray to God for you, that you faithfully wield the sword of God's word, — cut up all anti-christian remnants and men's inventions; that the gospel being rightly planted, may take an everlasting root among us and our posterity, to the glory of God and the increase of His kingdom, the discharge of your conscience, and the everlasting salvation of all his elect: which may He bring to pass for the sake of His crucified Jesus, to whom with the Holy Ghost be glory, now and forevermore. So be it. Your brother in the Lord Jesus, in whom I wish you as to mine own soul, and in whose name I do daily pray to God for you, with all His elect as for myself.

"W. WHITE."*

With equal boldness and fidelity White wrote to Bishop Grindal, desiring him to have "some remorse of conscience," and not to restrain the liberty he was once disposed to grant.

Is it possible, in view of the circumstances, to doubt the sincerity or the disinterestedness of these pioneers of religious liberty. They had nothing on earth to gain by their self-sacrificing course. There was no party in existence at the time to which they could look for sympathy or for succor. Yet it is plain that there was a power in their simple testimony that baffled the most learned and the strongest of their opponents. The impression made by their appeal to the word of God, did not indeed convince their adversaries, but in the irritation and vindictiveness so frequently betrayed, the involuntary proof was given that the prisoner, and not the judge, was in the right. And the loftiness of the confessor's principles is manifest in the eloquence with which they inspired his utterance of them.

* MSS. Part of a register.

II.

THE SEPARATISTS' FIRST PRINTER.

The principles held by the secret church in London were soon brought into considerable notoriety by the agency of the press, and a kind of ubiquitous agitation to which the chaplain of the Duke of Norfolk unexpectedly devoted himself. The prelates anxiously guarded the press. They had every thing to fear from the silent messengers that could penetrate into the dwellings of the people in all parts of the land, unaffected by the threatenings directed against oral teachers.

By a decree of the Star Chamber, issued June 29, 1566, unlicensed printing was prohibited under the severest penalties. Still, the men who had strong convictions to utter, found means to give them publicity in books and pamphlets. The vigilance of their adversaries was eluded by the printers and their supporters, by caution and ingenuity quite remarkable. Many of the aristocracy were on the side of the Puritans, and they afforded a shelter for ministers in the capacity of domestic chaplains. We may cite the case of John Brown, in the household of the Duchess of Suffolk, as an illustration. The mansion of her Grace stood nearly opposite the church of St. George the Martyr, in Southwark, and within it she gave shelter to the Puritan teacher. She had succored the martyrs in the days of Queen Mary, and she resolved to protect Christian confessors in the trying times of Elizabeth. With what firmness and tenacity she held her own against intimidation, we may infer from the following missive addressed to her on the 13th of January, 1571.

" Whereas, upon just cause, and according to the trust that Her Majesty hath put us in, we sent for one Brown, your Grace's chaplain (as he saith), by a messenger of Her Majesty's Chamber for that purpose. We are given to understand, that your Grace would not suffer him to come unto us, alleging a privileged place for his defence. Our commission extendeth to all places, as well exempt as not exempt, within Her Majesty's dominions; and before this time never by any called into question. We are persuaded that your Grace, knowing the authority of our commission, how straitly we are charged to proceed in redressing disorders, will not stay your said servant, contrary to the laws of this realm, but will send him unto us to answer such matter as he is charged withal. We would be loth to use other means to bring him to answer, as we must be forced to do, if your Grace will not like hereof. Thus we bid your Grace heartily farewell. From Lambeth, this 13th of January.

"Your loving friends,

"MATTHUE CANTUAR,
"ED. LOUDON,
"B. MONSON,
"GABRIEL GOODMAN,
"RICHARD WENDERSLEY."*

It was sufficiently mortifying to the official dignitaries to be baffled by a lady; but they could not help themselves. Her Grace of Suffolk stood so high, that they could not proceed against her with the reckless violence used so often toward the poor Separatists. The chaplain retained his place, and we find him, some years after, writing to Cartwright, "his very friend and brother in the Lord," on the subject of printing. "The cause of my writing," he says, "is to desire you to send me word whether we shall print where you have appointed. For I have found a good place in Southwark, at my brother Bradburne's, where we may do it, if you think good; for the Bishop of Winchester is gone into the country, and, so far as I know, he will not

---

* Petyt MS., Inner Temple, No. 47, fol. 507.

come again until the latter end of May. I was with my Lord of Bedford the fourth of this month, and he thinks it good that it were in Southwark." *

In order to print with safety, the managers of the press had to watch their opportunities, and, above all, to observe the movements of the bishops; but with care they succeeded in the attempt.

"In any of the great movements which have renewed the face of the world, or the condition of the human intellect, the multitude have never dispensed with a head. They look out for him not to get ideas, but because they have them; for, if they had not, they would not look for him. They seek him that he may act in accordance with these ideas, in order to realize them. Rather, they have no difficulty in finding him. The keenest, the strongest, not always the best or most enlightened, advances; sometimes advances quite alone and on his own account, but the standard which he raises soon gives him an army.

"Thus Luther advanced at first with a dubious and uncertain step. He carried with him, but in a more profound and distinct form, the obscure idea of a multitude. He spoke it aloud, and the multitude recognized it, recognized themselves; and through the perils of a dangerous war followed him

* Lansdowne MSS., Vol. 64, Art. 23.

who, so to speak, by a word made them acquainted with themselves." *

The people who separated themselves from the Establishment in England, found their man of action in Robert Browne. His position in society, as a relative of Lord Burghley, and the chaplain of the Duke of Norfolk, secured for him attention with some who might not have followed a leader of lowlier pretensions. He does not appear to have assumed the permanent care of a church, and in his checkered course he showed himself to be greatly deficient in the patience and stability requisite for the pastoral charge.

He struck out a path for himself, and went everywhere disseminating the views of church polity maintained by the brethren who had professed them before in obscurity and trial. Books written by him, in the exposition and defence of these principles, were widely circulated. Few men have expressed themselves on the subject more explicitly, or with greater clearness, than Robert Browne. "The church planted or gathered," he said, "is a company or number of Christians or believers, which, by a willing covenant made with their God, are under the government of God and Christ, and keep His laws in one holy communion; because Christ hath re-

* Vinet.

deemed them unto holiness and happiness forever, from which they were fallen by the sin of Adam. The church government is the Lordship of Christ in the communion of His offices; whereby His people yield obedience to His will, and have mutual use of their graces and callings to further their godliness and welfare."

"A pastor is a person having office and message of God, for exhorting and moving especially, and guiding accordingly, for the which he is tried to be meet, and thereto is duly chosen by the church which calleth him, or received by obedience where he planteth the church."

It is difficult, in the light of the nineteenth century, to imagine what possible harm could arise from such principles, defended as they were only by plain and pertinent quotations from Scripture. The prelates of the Anglican Church, however, viewed them in a different light, as dangerous both to Church and State. The death penalty was not thought too severe to be inflicted on those who maintained them. John Copping and Elias Thacker, two ministers of Suffolk, were arraigned for the offence of circulating the writings of Browne. Copping, on the accusation of nonconformity, was thrown into prison in 1576, and still holding fast to his integrity, on a reëxamination, Dec. 1, 1578, he was sent back to prison, where he remained five years longer with his companion Thacker. Finally, they were brought up before the authorities in 1583, and in the month of June were put to death at Bury St. Edmunds, in conformity with the Statute of 23 Eliz. William Dennis of Thetford, in Norfolk, suffered martyrdom for the same cause.

Robert Browne, no doubt, would have had to sacrifice his life, but for the powerful intervention of Lord Burghley. As it was, and with all the influence exerted in his favor, he was spared only on condition of an ignominious silence. The position he took, in consequence, was in every way unfavorable for his reputation. The prelatical party, disappointed of their prey, affixed the name of Brownist to the Separatists, as a standing reproach. The consistent adherents to the principles advocated by Browne, could only regard him as a deserter; though there is no evidence that he sought actively to oppose the doctrines he had zealously taught. From a curious entry in the parochial records of St. Olaves, Southwark, we are able to determine his exact relations. The following entries will show his humiliating condition:

"*Item*. The 31st day of November, 1586, was chosen to be schoolmaster Robert Browne, upon his good behavior, and observing these articles hereunder written:

"*First*. That you shall not intermeddle with the

minister, or disturb the quiet of the parishioners, by keeping any conventicles or conference with any suspected or disorderly persons.

"*Secondly.* That you shall bring your children to sermons and lectures in the church, and there accompany them for their better government.

"*Thirdly.* If any error shall be found in you, and you convinced thereof, that you shall, upon admonition thereof, revoke it, and conform yourself to the doctrine of the Church of England.

"*Fourthly.* You shall read in your school no other catechism than is authorized by public authority.

"*Fifthly.* That you shall, at convenient times, communicate in this parish according to the laws.

"*Sixthly.* Not being contented to answer and keep these articles, no longer to keep the schoolmastership, but to avoid it.

"Subscribed by me, Robert Browne, according to my answers before all the governors, and the distinctions and exceptions before them named."

There is an inherent vitality in the truth, by which it is continued through all changes, rising superior to every obstacle, and prevailing over its enemies, and, what is more remarkable, advancing in its course, notwithstanding the defection of friends.

The cause of the Separatists had sustained what appeared to be a most signal defeat. The great Puritan party had also suffered from the violence of persecution, and to meet the storm they were compelled to act with extreme caution. They retained their places in the establishment wherever it was practicable, but formed a church within a church, to avoid the practical inconsistency of recognizing the mixed multitude in a parochial assembly, as a company of true Christian believers. The zeal of the Separatists created difficulties in this temporizing policy, and the leaders of the party did not conceal their displeasure. The sister-in-law of Cartwright (Mrs. Stubbs) was induced to join the society of the Separatists, though deprived of ministerial instruction. Her conduct, in this particular, was strongly disapproved by her brother. She could pretend to no polemical skill, like that which had been practised in so many theological encounters. Yet, notwithstanding the disparity in their controversial ability, Mrs. Stubbs was ready to give a reason for her choice and Christian practice.

"I am moved, sister, by the mutual bond between us," said Cartwright, "to use some persuasion with you to communicate with us in the worship of God."

Sister. The people of God are a peculiar people to the Lord, and we may not join with those who do not obey the will of Christ. Moreover, the Lord is one, and the people of God cannot be divided, some with and some not with Him.

Cartwright. As if your unity with Christ and

separation from all who are without were not here imperfect, and only to be perfected when Christ shall make a final separation between the sheep and the goats. You have not yet proved that we are the Babylonians, from whom you, the only Jews forsooth in the world, are bound to separate.

Sister. You are not the church, not being formed in obedience to the law of Christ.

Cartwright. Our obedience is imperfect, so is also our faith; and therefore we are not to be shut from the church for our defective obedience.

Sister. I believe; Lord, help mine unbelief. But what is this to your presumptuous sins and wilful breach of the law of God.

Cartwright. The prophet prayed in his presumptuous sins.

Sister. You do unjustly wrest the truth. I am commanded by the Lord to come out from among them that are not of the church of God, by agreement of His word. In that you obey not, but resist the word of Christ; neither have you the authority to bind and loose. The church of God do elect ministers by the free choice of the people of God. Every one in godliness and sobriety is to have his free choice, and not to have it thrust upon them.

Cartwright. Most of our ministers are chosen by the people.

Sister. Some do allow this, and some do not.

Cartwright. That order is taken from the custom in the commonwealth, and the most voices do prevail.

Sister. I think this to be an odd reason by the word of God.

Cartwright. All churches of God say we are a church of God.

Sister. This is the praise of men, and not of God. There is no separation in your churches. A great number of both ministers and people have no knowledge in the true faith; and you do not come out from among them. This is the separation I mean. You have not the power of Christ to excommunicate any by the lords your bishops; and thence cometh even the power of antichrist. It must needs be Christ or Antichrist. I know it is not Christ by his word.

Cartwright. Remember your frailty as a woman, and the small ordinary means of discerning exactly the truth. You have not the truth, because it is not taught you by some pastor under Christ.

Sister. It is taught by our Saviour Christ and his apostles, and believed of us, and the Lord will comfortably teach us one of another, if He see good and most to ·His own glory. I humbly beseech Him that He will bring us together, that we may lead a quiet and peaceable life in all godliness and honesty, according to the sweet course of the gospel; and I pray God that we may ever love the truth, and increase in the knowledge and obedience thereof, howsoever we be separated, yea, although we are counted as sheep to the slaughter.

Cartwright. You are not a church, because there are not among you that have the knowledge of the tongues wherein the Scriptures are written; so you cannot refute the adversaries.

Sister. The Scriptures of God are not like men's words; for no man knoweth the mind of a man but himself. We see our hearts in the word of God; and I think some of the churches of God have the knowledge of tongues. But consider your own ministers. The Word saith, not some learned among them, but the minister, howsoever your own ministers judge in the matter. Truly my heart mourneth to see the general hardness of heart, when we speak to any that standeth with you. The word of God can take no place. You have so strengthened them in their sins, saying, Peace, peace. You can do no way so much evil as to call them the church of God, when, according to His word, you still stand without.

Cartwright. I marvel to see the veil of ignorance that is over your hearts. You can say nothing to my words.

Sister. Truly I thank the Lord, to whom be all the glory. I do not pass for man's judgment. I open unto the Lord in obeying His truth, so far as I know, with all my heart. I marvel that you say I answer nothing to your words. I should gladly rejoice to see you profess the truth in uprightness of heart."

The style of these close and earnest colloquies is a little too quaint for the modern reader, and we fear to extend them further, lest we should weary attention; but we know of no method so suited to exhibit the heart-life of the people, in whose history we are interested, as to listen to their conversation. Few, comparatively, clearly understand the distinction between the Puritans, and the Separatists who gave rise to the Pilgrim fathers. We must introduce two interlocutors of the olden time to talk over the matter. If their tone should not be agreeable, we must excuse the reader, in the expectation of meeting him in the next chapter. One of these worthies, after the fashion of his day, calls himself "Desiderius;" the other is "Miles Micklebound."

Desid. It is sorrow enough that you prefer the Brownists before our Puritan ministers.

Miles. I have good reason in this case so to do. For as they hold it unlawful for our ministers of England to have their idolatrous livings, so they hold it unlawful for their own and all other livings to have them; but would that they were returned to the commonwealth, from whence they were taken. But our Puritan ministers, that wish the prelates down, and their livings taken from them, would gladly have them for their own use, as you likewise pleaded for them; and I fear they hold it no better than sacrilege, if they be otherwise employed. I can show you divers ways whereby you may discern that the Brownists (as you call them) are the best champions to fight the battle, and are most likely to win the field.

Desid. I cannot tell. I am sure they are counted a sect, and are everywhere evil spoken of.

Miles. But the question is, whether it is for evil doing, or for well doing? If for well doing, they are to bear it patiently, as partakers of the cross and sufferings of Christ, whose faithful servants and witnesses of old, even the sect of the Nazarenes, were everywhere evil spoken of in like sort. But did it therefore follow, that they were according to the report and esteem that was among men concerning them? Or should men therefore have rejected them, or any good among them? Let it be far from you so to think; and further off, in that sort to speak of those former, or yet of these later Christians. Christ himself was the chief corner stone, whom the builders refused, yet became the head of the corner. And surely these men, which you and others are ready enough to refuse for help in this sorrow, are the most sound and sufficient of any that I know for convicting our common adversaries and terrible opposites, the prelates and lofty clergy of the land. Wherefore I would advise you and all never to shun, but diligently to seek, and thankfully to receive their help when it may be had; and if we see them to err in any other thing (as all men are subject to error), let readiness be showed in the spirit of meekness to help them. Thus shall we both please God and comfort one another.

Desid. Therein you say well. But they condemn (as the report goes) not only the best people of the land; but also condemn and forsake the faith professed and maintained here, counting it the faith of devils, and professing other faith for themselves.

Now for my own part, I am not only persuaded, but fully assured, through the mercy of God, that the faith professed in England, is the true saving faith of God's elect; and if ever they be saved themselves, it must be through the same faith in Christ. Therefore, if they be guilty of that report, my soul shall have no pleasure in them till they return by repentance. For to err in that point is a matter of no small importance.

Miles. That report is either a mere slander raised up of the devil in his instruments for the disgrace of their cause, or if ever it was spoken by any of them, it must be some one very simple, that erreth therein through ignorance, or some that are strongly carried with zeal against the false and confused order of the church; and not distinguishing between order and faith, may happen through haste or inconsiderateness, to call the one by the name of the other, and so, when they speak of the impure faith of the Church of England, may intend only the impure and corrupt order that is therein.

Desid. If you had not holpen with such a lift, they had lain under it for me. But sure such zeal is preposterous zeal, and such inconsiderateness is heady, rash, and indiscreet carriage, not agreeing with Christianity, not beseeming sobriety.

Miles. Be it so. Yet can you not justly impute that to a whole company which is done by one or two, where the rest do not approve it, but are against it. And there is no religion wherein there are not some that miscarry themselves, either through zeal or ignorance, or else in heady, rash, and inconsiderate speech. Yet such, as so offend among these, are liable to the rebuke of the whole Presbytery and church itself, if the case so require, and the main difference between them and the Church of England is about outward orders and ordinances, and the faith possessed by both is one and the same.

Desid. Wherefore are the chief defenders of this cause called Brownists?

Miles. Because one Mr. Browne, minister at a

church in Northamptonshire, heretofore professed their cause, published it in press, and for a time continued the practice of it, till the fear of persecution and love of this world, like Demas, or of ease like Issachar, made him to turn his back upon it; and yet I think (if he were asked), his conscience will not suffer his tongue to say, that it is not the truth, although he hath left the relief of Sion to live upon the spoils of Babylon.

Desid. Were there none that did write for the cause before Brown.

Miles. Yes, verily, the prophets, apostles, and Evangelists, have in their authentic writings laid down the ground thereof, and upon that ground is all their building reared up, and surely settled. Moreover, many of the martyrs, both former and later have maintained it, as is to be seen in the acts and monuments of the church. The separated church, whereof Mr. Fitz was pastor, professed and practised that cause, before Mr. Brown wrote for it. But he being one of the first writers in Her Majesty's realm, therefore those that followed him (or Christ rather, through his means directing them by God's word) were called Brownists, as if they had been baptized into his name, which were falsehood to think, and blasphemy to speak.

Desid. The name makes them very odious to others, and, to say the truth, it caused me to carry some prejudice against them, to the forestalling of my judgment in the things they hold.

Miles. There are many that do so, but let not the name offend you or any; for there was never any truth brought to light, but Satan, through his notable craft and cunning, hath caused some to paint it out after the names of men, that it might seem base and contemptible in the eyes of all, and to be received of none. Hereupon have Christians been called Hussites, Huguenots, Lutherans, Zuinglians, Calvinists, Puritans, Brownists, and the like, but there could be no name more odious than was given to our Master Christ himself, whom the wicked called Beelzebub, and his people must (in their measure) be partaker of His reproach. Let none therefore seek to have a good name by doing any evil thing, nor yet, for avoiding a bad name, neglect any good that God requires at our hands; neither let any man measure any truth by the face that foes do set upon it.

Desid. I perceive by your plea, that if these men had their right, they would be acknowledged for true Christians, and not be calumniated by the name of Brownists.

Miles. Your perceiving then is good, and your words are just and right, for so they ought to be esteemed.

Desid. But why then do you so often call them so yourself?

Miles. For distinction's sake only, but not at all in reproach; and if you could always understand me, whom I mean when I call them Christians, then would I give them no other name.

Desid. What difference do you put between those people called Brownists, and the sincerest and best professors of the Gospel called Puritans?

Miles. The difference is laid down in few words. The former do both hold and practise the truth, and separate themselves from the contrary. The latter have the truth in speculation only, and either dare not, or at least do not, practise it. They neither dare, nor do they leave off all the unrighteous ordinances of antichrist.

Desid. Some do object against them, their manner of receiving the Lord's Supper, as being rude, irreverent, malapert, and too presumptuous, — sitting upon their seats as if they were Christ's comrades; whereas for more reverence they ought to take it kneeling.

[Miles is taking out his New Testament to defend the practice of sitting at the Lord's table by various examples; but as the discussion throws no further light upon our subject, we must leave it with him and his friend Desiderius to finish at their leisure.]

III.

THE PURITANS AND SEPARATISTS.

Having had the distinction between a Puritan and a Brownist explained to us by Miles Nicklebound, it may aid us to better understand the course of the Hidden Church, if we glance at the relative position of parties at this critical juncture.

The Puritans were a formidable body, when in 1572 they formed the first English Presbytery at Wansworth (a retired village on the banks of the Thames, and four miles from London), and submitted their scheme of church discipline to parliament. Their leaders, eminent for piety and learning, were held in high esteem by the continental reformers. Many of the nobility adopted their opinions and valued their ministerial services. The citizens of London flocked in crowds to hear them preach, so long as they retained their pulpits, and when, with their brethren in the provinces, they were silenced and put under the ban, earnest petitions were sent by men of the best social position in the country, pleading for their restoration to the churches from which they had been expelled. The spirit of the people may be inferred from the "supplication," sent by the parishioners of Aldermary, in the city of London. They say, "of late we to our comfort did enjoy Mr. Field to be our preacher, who labored painfully among us, for the space of four years, in preaching the word of God, and catechizing our youth, teaching obedience both to God and our prince, and keeping us in good order. Since his restraint and inhibition, we are left as scattered sheep upon the mountains, and have none ordinarily to break unto us the bread of life; than which a greater evil cannot come upon us. We feel persuaded, that if the matter be fully examined, there will be found in him no cause why he should be sequestered from us. For we are able to witness, even in the presence of Him who seeth all hearts, that to our knowledge he ever behaved himself wisely and faithfully, as became a true minister of Jesus Christ. The things urged against him were never hindered, impugned, or in any way resisted by him, but were duly kept and preserved. And seeing that which he received was out of our purses, without any burden upon the church whatever, we cannot help feeling ourselves hardly treated, that, without cause, he should be taken from us." *

* MS. Register, p. 285.

Fuller says of the early Puritans, "What won them most repute was their ministers' painful preaching, it being observed in England, that those who hold the helm of the pulpit, always stir the people's heart as they please."

To this growing moral resistance on the part of the people to their arbitrary measures, the hierarchy opposed enactments of greater severity. Whitgift, who was called the "black husband" of the queen, could always rely on the utmost stretch of the royal prerogative to support his plans of coercion. Independent representatives in parliament, who protested against his measures, were arrested and kept in prison at the pleasure of the court. When the laws failed to supply the fitting instrument of repression, a proclamation was issued to improvise mandates, having the force of statutes, without their formality. The imperious will of Elizabeth secured for the prelates an ascendency which no combination, secret or open, could prevent.

The struggle of the Puritans against their ecclesiastical opponents, for a time, was conducted with great energy and skill; but gradually they were broken, and so disheartened that they sank helplessly into the shade.

Bishop Horn, reporting the triumph of the crosier, says the "mischievous men who drew the people into what they called purity, are now silenced, skulk about, and are become of no importance."

The cedars were broken, but the vine still found room to grow.

"When man would raise upon earth something to shade him, or to shelter him, see what preparations, what materials, scaffolding, and workmen, what hewing and digging, and heaps of rubbish. But God, when it so pleases him, takes the smallest grain of seed that a new-born babe could grasp in its tiny hand, puts it into the bosom of the earth; and from this grain, which lies at first unnoticed, produces that immense tree, beneath whose shade the families of mankind may find shelter. The doing of great things by imperceptibly small means, such is the rule with God." *

A more feeble, or a more despised people, than the Separatists of the sixteenth century, it would be difficult to find, except in the primitive Christians, who were regarded as the "filth and offscouring of all things." But indeed they were far weaker than the members of the apostolic churches. At the time of which we are writing, they had no leaders either to instruct them, or to vindicate their cause. The contempt of the proud was upon them without stint,

* Merle D'Aubigne.

and every one who had the desire to keep a decent reputation, shunned them as the plague. We have seen that, by the term separation, they meant no more than the inspired apostle, when he said, "Be ye separate;" but their adversaries insisted on separating them as rigid schismatics, who would recognize neither truth nor piety, except within their own narrow circles.

There were no ancient monuments of past glory to which they could point like the Roman Catholics; they had no friends of distinction at home, or in foreign countries, from whom they could receive either success or the assurances of fraternal sympathy; but poor, tried, and afflicted, they stood alone, and were not reckoned as of any account by any parties. Yet, beneath the eye of the good Shepherd, they went forward in faith and hope.

Their track is so obscure at this period that they would be lost altogether to our view, if they had not been at intervals surprised in their meetings for worship. The suburbs of London were to a great extent covered with woods. Here and there plots of ground were enclosed as gardens to supply the markets of the city. The Separatists found in some of the owners, friends who were ready to receive them to the "garden house" for worship, in the colder months of the year; and in summer they left their homes, early on the Sabbath morning, to meet in some sequestered dell to read the Scriptures, offer their free and unpremeditated comments, and unite in fervent prayer. The simple repast of which they partook in common was scarcely an interruption, and so they spent the day, returning in the evening, after making a collection for the relief of their brethren in bonds.

IV.

SEPARATIST PRINCIPLES FROM THE PRISONS.

"Where do you assemble?" said Prefect Rusticius to Justin Martyr. "Wherever," replied Justin, "it suits each one's preference and ability. You take for granted that we all meet in the same place; but it is not so, for the God of the Christians is not circumscribed by place, but, being invisible, fills heaven and earth, and is everywhere worshiped and glorified by the faithful." Rusticius then said, "Tell me where you meet together, or in what place you collect your disciples?" Justin said: "I am staying at the house of one Martinus, and I know of no other place of worship besides; if any one wished to come to me, I communicated to him the words of truth."

This example of the church in the house is only one of innumerable instances to be found in times of persecution. Every place, to those who worship God in spirit and in truth, is hallowed ground.

Let us turn to an interesting scene in the baronial hall at Rochford in Essex. Lord Rich and his family, with the servants of the household, are assembled for evening prayers. The company is somewhat larger than we usually find in a domestic establishment. Several of the poorer neighbors are present and sitting amongst them. We see Mr. Butler of Tooby, Lord Grey, and other members of aristocratic families in the vicinity. Prayer is offered by Mr. Wright, the Puritan chaplain, assisted by Mr. Greenwood, B. A. The servants are catechized, an expository lecture is given, and it is intimated by Lord Rich that all present, who are sincere believers in Christ, may have an opportunity to form themselves into a church under the pastoral care of Mr. Wright.

This incident, in 1580, as regards John Greenwood, may be regarded as a transitionary step from the Puritans to the Separatists. Robert Wright, from the time of leaving Cambridge, had never felt satisfied with the Anglican order of service, and to obtain ordination, more scriptural in his view, he went to Antwerp, and joined Cartwright and other Puritans in the church, of which Secretary Davison was an elder. After a brief ministry at Vilvord, he returned to his native country, but the service to which he was invited, by Lord Rich, he requested to decline, for want, as he said, "of audacity and utterance."

The Bishop of London was greatly incensed on hearing of the services to which we have referred, and complained bitterly that he could not come by "Wright, sheltered in the house of Lord Rich, unless he sent a power of men to pull him out by the ears." Ultimately, the Bishop succeeded in his purpose, and while he sent Wright to the Fleet, he committed Lord Rich to the Marshalsea. The sufferings of Wright broke his spirit. On the 11th of September, 1582, the Bishop, in a letter to Lord Burghley, says: "Whereas Mr. Wright, now a prisoner in the Gatehouse, hath willingly subscribed to the good allowance of the Ministry of England, and the book of common prayer (as I take it), unto which both points, if he can be content with his friends, to stand bound in a good round sum, that, from henceforth, he shall neither commit in writing, or preach any thing contrary to the same; I, for my part, do not mislike that he shall have some favor, so that Her Majesty be privy thereunto."*

What happened to the ministerial associate of Wright, under these circumstances, we do not learn; but one thing is certain, the trials and changes to which his patron and friend were subjected, did not move him from his steadfastness. When we last saw him it was in the mansion of a Christian nobleman, and engaged in service perfectly congenial.

* Lansdowne MS., Vol. 36, art. 19, p. 141.

We turn now to another scene, and one entirely contrasted. On the south bank of the Thames, and near the foot of London Bridge, stood the palace of the Bishop of Winchester, and at the end of an adjoining park was the prison, used by the bishop for the subjugation of persons of refractory conscience, as well as for other purposes. The kennel for his dogs was kept in a far less offensive condition. Enter through the iron gate and look into this wretched dungeon. The stench is odious, the air is pestilential, and the filthiness of every part of it most revolting, but all this is as nothing in comparison with the diseased and abandoned people who have been crammed within its walls. There they lie huddled together in litters of straw, felons, murderers, maniacs, men and women of the vilest character, without order and without discipline, and amongst them, though not of them, stands the scholar, the Christian, the faithful and devoted minister, John Greenwood.

Will he then be forgotten and forsaken? Will none of his old college companions inquire after his welfare, or again recognize him as one of their fraternity? The Sabbath morning dawns upon that dreary cell (Nov. 19, 1586), and with it are connected associations sacred and delightful, notwithstanding the horrid spectacle around him, and Greenwood thinks of hours spent in earnest discourse, and in more fervent prayer with his faithful brother, Henry Barrowe.

A loud knock at the prison gate, followed by a message from the turnkey to announce that "Barrowe is come to visit his friend," awakens in the breast of the prisoner the joy that is caused only by such acts of constancy and kindness.

The interview and mutual greeting, too touching for description, we pass over, to recite, in their order, subsequent occurrences.

The faithful brethren were not suffered long to express to each other the sentiments of Christian affection, and, like David and Jonathan, to strengthen their hands in God.

" You are my prisoner, Mr. Barrowe," said Shephard, the jailer, and turning to his assistants he added, in a tone of authority, " order the boat."

Barrowe was taken off without delay, and soon found himself sailing in the custody of pursuivants on the Thames to Lambeth. There was little time for explanation, and the jailer of the Clink cared less to give it, from the assurance that he would have perfect indemnity. The party landed at the palace, passed quickly through the gateway, and over the beautiful lawn, to the hall in which they found the archbishop sitting on the bench with the assistant commissioners. The prisoner was commanded to kneel and to answer such questions on oath, concerning his own conduct, as might be put to him. To the oath he demurred, and one of those strange inquisitions was entered into, so common on such occasions.

Barrowe was connected with an aristocratic family, well known at the court, and he had been a student for the legal profession at Gray's Inn. He told the archbishop that they were acquainted with each other at Cambridge, but he received no courtesy on this account.

For the few hours he was detained at Lambeth, he would probably occupy the strong room in the Lollard's tower, on the walls of which the iron rings still remain to which the chains of the martyrs were fastened in the preceding reign. He might read for his comfort and support the words of Scripture, written by them when called to suffer for the testimony of Jesus. He was sent to prison, and then brought up with Greenwood for reëxamination; not so much to convict them of any offence, as to squeeze out their consciences, and to reduce them to the common spiritual vassalage in which Puritan leaders were now enthralled.

For six long years this experiment was tried. Protracted torture was inflicted, with alternations of tantalizing relief, that they might be compelled to regulate their convictions according to the decrees of the high commission.

They were closely watched in prison, and deprived as far as possible of all means and facilities for the communication of their sentiments. Yet, by stealth they found opportunity to put down their thoughts on scraps of paper, which were given to Cicely, the servant of Mr. Greenwood, or to others who brought them food, and then sent by a faithful Christian friend to Holland to be printed. What can we expect as to the evenness of style or niceties of expression, in books written under such extreme difficulties?

Their treatises probably will never be reprinted. We must therefore be indulged in giving a few extracts to indicate the spirit of the men.

"We profess," they say, "the same faith and truth of the gospel, which all the reformed churches this day do hold and maintain. We go beyond them in the detestation of all popery, and draw nearer, in some points, unto Christ's holy order and institution."

They recognized no human infallibility, either in churches or in individual Christians. "What can be more miserable," they ask, "than to see with other men's eyes, and to believe with other men's hearts." Of Calvin they said, "We are not to be blamed if we suffer ourselves to be pressed with, or to follow his writings no further than they are found consonant with the word of God."

"The word of God is the archetype and groundwork of all states, degrees, and actions, both ecclesiastical and civil, whereby they must be framed, whereby they shall be judged; no other thing standing before the face of the great Judge than His own revealed will in His word."

They disclaimed all intention to effect a reformation by external force. "Private members, however they ought to refrain and to keep their souls and bodies undefiled from all false worship which is imposed, suffering in all patient and Christian manner whatsoever may be inflicted for the same (as they that fear more to offend God than men); yet ought they not to stretch forth their hand by force to the reformation of any public enormities, which, by the magistrates, are set up. Yet it is the bounden duty of every true-hearted subject and faithful servant of God to witness and cry out against all things that are exalted against the knowledge of God."

The course of the Christian, under hostile rulers was, in their view, to be that of patient endurance. "Obedience must always be in the Lord. If the prince demand or command my body or my goods in his service, I am to obey them both readily; only I am to look to the outward thing which I do, that it be lawful and warranted by the word. If not so, I may not obey, but rather his indignation, yea death itself."

Of the church, they write: "God commandeth private men to set up the discipline which Christ hath left. The faithful are commanded to gather together in Christ's name, with promise of direction and protection; and not only to establish His laws and ordinances among them, but faithfully to govern His church thereby.

"No prince or mortal man can make any man a member of a church.

"The Lord calleth them to believe and lay hold of Christ Jesus as their alone Saviour; to honor and obey Him, as their anointed King, Priest, and Prophet; to submit themselves unto Him in all things; to be reformed, corrected, and governed, and directed by His most holy word, vowing their faithful obedience unto the same, as that shall be revealed unto them. By this faith, confession, and profession, every member of Christ, from the greatest unto the least, without respect of persons, entereth into and standeth in the church.

"The prince himself entereth into the church, and is bound to the strict observation and obedience of God's laws, in his calling, as well as any other; and is, for any transgression thereof, liable and subject to the censures and judgments of Christ in His church, which are without partiality or respect of persons; which censures and judgments, if the prince contemn, he contemneth against his own soul, and is, therefore, by the same power of Christ, to be disfranchised out of the church. Though by this sin he loseth his right to be a Christian, or a member of his church, yet loseth he not his right to be a king or a magistrate, and is so to be held and obeyed of all faithful Christians who are His subjects.

"Into the church entereth no profane, ignorant, or ungodly person.

"Every particular congregation, being a faithful flock, destitute of some minister, for example of a pastor, ought to make choice of some faithful Christian, of whose virtues, knowledge, judgment, fitness, and conversation, according to the rules in that behalf prescribed (1 Tim. iii.; Titus i.; Acts xiv.), they have assured proof and experience in some Christian congregation or other where he hath lived. Such a one, the whole congregation being gathered together in the name of God, with fasting and prayer for the especial guidance of His Holy Spirit, to be directed to that person whom the Lord hath made meet, and appointed for that high character and ministry. In which election every particular member of the said congregation hath his particular interest of assent or dissent, showing his reasons of dissent in reverent manner, not disturbing the holy and peaceable order of the church.

"This choice thus made, accepted, and determined, the elect is to be publicly ordained and received, and of the same congregation whereof and whereunto he is chosen.

"The true ministry should be maintained of the free, yet dutiful benevolence of the faithful, especially of that flock unto which they attend and minister, according to the present ability of the one and needs of the other. The true sheep and faithful people of Christ will not only bestow their earthly good, but even their lives, for those that bring unto them these heavenly treasures; that tread out the corn and divide the portion unto them that labor for and watch over their souls."

Again we must remind the reader, that these prison thoughts were recorded in a place that combined with the restraints of a dungeon the contagion of a pest-house, the vice of a brothel, and the distractions of bedlam. Yet what purity and moral sublimity of sentiment, what an equal balance of correlative duties, what a sense of the beauty of order, what calmness and what power!

It was under such teaching that our fathers were nerved for the conflict, and strengthened to endure. We may imagine how inspiring, for example, they felt the words of Barrowe to be, when they anticipated the time for the organization of a Christian church; the act so simple and so scriptural, and yet so fiercely denounced as one of blind temerity and of ecclesiastical crime. The prisons, in which these noble-minded confessors wrote, have long since been levelled with the dust. A few unsightly and blackened ruins alone remain of the palace of the Bishop of Winchester, in whose custody they were held. But these words will live, and the names of the men who uttered them will be cherished in grateful remembrance in coming ages, and by multitudes inhabiting regions then unknown. We return to the narrative.

It occurred to the bishops in council that a system of periodical visitation of the Separatists in prison, conducted by the clergy of the city, in rotation, would be useful, either to bring them to submission, or to glean evidence to be produced against them in the event of trial. Their scheme will appear in the letter of instructions we subjoin:

"To our loving friends, Mr. Archdeacon Mullins, Doctor Andros, Mr. Cotton, Mr. Hutchinson, and the rest of the preachers within named after our hearty commendations:

"I, the Bishop of London, have received order from my Lord's Grace of Canterbury, with the advice of both the chief justices, that conference should presently be had with these sectaries which do forsake our church, and be for the same committed prisoners; for that it is intended, if by our good and learned persuasions they will not be reduced to conform themselves to their dutiful obedience, that they shall be proceeded with, all according to the course of common law.

" Wherefore these are to will and require you, and every one of you whose names are mentioned (forty-three in number) in the schedule hereunto annexed, in Her Majesty's name, and by virtue of her high commission for causes ecclesiastical to us and others directed; that twice every week (at the least) you do repair to those persons and prisoners (fifty-two in number) whose names are in the ticket set down, and that you seek by all learned and discreet demeanor you may, to reduce them from their errors; and for that either their conformity or disobedience may be made manifest when they shall come unto their trial. Therefore we require you to set down in writing, the particular days of your going to confer with them, and likewise your censure what it is of them; as that, if occasion do serve to use it, you will be sworn unto; and for that Dr. Stanhope, chancellor to me, the Bishop of London, is gone out of the city, therefore we require Mr. Mullins to send for all those several preachers, and deliver the names of the prisoners, together with the prisons whereunto they are assigned to resort, and to require them as aforesaid to take the charge upon them, according to the trust committed unto them; and in case any of them refuse, that then you require him or them forthwith to repair to me to Fulham, and to certify me of their answers before their coming, and so we bid you farewell, the 25th of Feb., 1589.

"Your loving friends,
"JOHN LOUD,
"JOHN HERBERT,
"EDW. STANHOPE,
"RICHARD COSEN."

The duties imposed on these clerical detectives were not the most inviting, especially to any of them who might retain the sense of Christian honor. To act the spy, under the pretence of a visit for the spiritual benefit of the prisoner, was not what would be at all agreeable to men who would not lose self-respect. But they knew well what was meant by the alternative, "to repair" to the Lord Bishop at Fulham, — and they went to their degrading task.

We shall not follow them through all their rounds. A mere glimpse will be sufficient to show the prisoner and visitor in contrast. Mr. Hutchinson is appointed to confer with John Greenwood. They meet; but who can describe the peculiar expression of countenance with which they exchange salutations. Greenwood seems to have some suspicion of the errand of his visitor, and stipulates that Mr. Calthorpe, a gentleman in the prison, may be present as witness, and that he may be furnished with pen, ink, and paper to note down the questions and replies. These literary luxuries for once are allowed.

Before the conference, Mr. Hutchinson gave a memorandum to the effect that "he did not examine Mr. Greenwood in any way to hurt him, but to confer with him about his separating himself from the Church of England." Greenwood, on his part, prepared a note to state that "he did not desire Mr. Hutchinson's company, but was most willing of any Christian conference."

These preliminaries being settled, the polemical duel began.

"All the people," said Greenwood, "by the blowing of Her Majesty's trumpet at her coronation, were in one day received without conversion of life by faith and repentance, and they and their children generally received to your sacrament without separation from the world. They could not, therefore, be ἐκκλησία — a people called out."

Hutchinson replied: "I know not what you mean by separation."

"You know," Greenwood rejoined, "what בדל *badal* signifieth; and as light is separated from darkness, so must the church from the profane."

These few sentences will give you an idea of the manner in which the visitors were met. They took care not to subject themselves to the noxious effluvia of the prison.

When Dr. Andros accompanied Mr. Hutchinson to examine Barrowe, the prisoner was sent for to meet them in the parlor of the keeper, attended by three servants.

"Your chamber-fellow, Mr. Greenwood, hath told you the cause of our coming," said Mr. Hutchinson, blandly.

Barrowe. "He told me that some had been with him yesternight, but told me not the cause of your coming unto me this day."

Hutchinson. "We come to the same end to confer brotherly with you, concerning certain positions that you are said to hold."

Barrowe. "I deserve nothing more than Christian conference, but having been two years and wellnigh a half kept by the bishops in close prison, could never as yet obtain any such conference where the Book of God might peaceably decide all our controversies."

Dr. Andros, in rather a simpering manner, offered the prisoner his congratulations on his close confinement: "For close imprisonment you are most happy; the solitary and contemplative life I hold the most blessed life. It is the life I would choose."

Barrowe. "You speak philosophically, but not christianly. So sweet is the harmony of God's graces to me in the congregation and the conversation of the saints at all times, that I think myself as a sparrow on the house-top when I am exiled from them. But could you be content also, Mr. Andros, to be kept from exercise and air so long together? These are also necessary to a natural body."

Barrowe made no complaint, as he might have done, of the "facinorous wretches" that would disturb the most philosophic contemplations.

Andros. "I say not that I would want air. But who be those saints that you speak of, — where are they?"

Barrowe — waxing rather warm at the stoicism of his inquisitor — said: "They are even those poor Christians whom you so blaspheme and persecute, and now most unjustly hold in your prisons."

Andros. "But where is their congregation?"

Barrowe. "Though I knew, I purposed not to tell you."

Hutchinson, disappointed in his object, became excited, and said: "They are a company of sectaries, as you also are."

Barrowe quickly asked: "Know you what a sectary is?"

A discussion arose on the Latin and Greek roots, during which a lexicon was sent for; but Dr. Andros, finding it inconvenient to meet Barrowe on the point, changed the subject.

"Order," said the doctor, "requireth that you should rather begin to dispute about the ministry first."

Barrowe observed: "There must be a sheep before there can be a flock, and a flock before there is a shepherd."

Andros replied: "A flock and a shepherd are relatives."

Barrowe reiterated the sentiment: "There must be a flock before there can be a shepherd, because the people must choose the pastor."

Subsequently, when Greenwood was present, the old taunt was repeated as to sects: "Sects," said one of the visitors, "are understood of such Brownists and schismatics as you are."

Barrowe replied: "It is your custom to bless Christ's enemies and blaspheme Christ's servants. We are no Brownists. We hold not our faith in respect of any mortal man; neither were we instructed by him, or baptized into his name, until by such as you we were so termed. Schismatics we are not. We hold communion with all Christian servants in true faith and love, only we have separated ourselves from the false church and false ministry which we have found you to be."

Greenwood offered, in substance, the same disclaimer: "Browne is an apostate, now one of your church. You receive all such apostates from Christ.

We never had any thing to do with Browne, neither are we members of your church."

The visitors returned to make their report; and Barrowe, with his companion Greenwood, also made known their state to Lord Burghley.

V.

ELECTION OF CHURCH OFFICERS.

The detachment of the persecuted company of Christian believers, meeting in the fields and woods, from the religious teachers of their time, seems to have been necessary to prepare them for the examination of first principles as contained in the New Testament. It was scarcely possible for men who had been trained in the ecclesiastical systems, formed under the influence of national establishments, to escape from traditional and conventional peculiarities. They were so accustomed to artificial supports for the church, that they had the feeling of men who supposed the sky must fall unless pillars were raised by the hand of man to keep it in its position. The "fewest of all people," and the meanest in worldly estimation, were chosen in Providence to form the Christian church after the primitive model, pure and simple as on the day the Lord Jesus ascended into heaven. Ministers were raised up to take the oversight of them, who had received the highest intellectual training; but not until their original clerical pretensions had been broken down, like the pharisaic pride of Saul of Tarsus, by the force of truth and outward discipline of the severest nature. The seed-corn was but a handful, made still less by the process of winnowing.

If a stranger could have witnessed the humble gathering of people in the house of Roger Rippon in Southwark, or at the dwelling of "one Fox" in Nicolas Lane, met for the solemnities of an ordination, he must have been struck with their peculiar simplicity.

In 1592, the brethren were convened to complete their church organization. The probability is, that several meetings were held for this purpose in different places besides those just mentioned, amongst others at " Mr. Lee's," near Smithfield, " in a house near Aldgate," and in a garden-house at St. George's in the Fields.

The doors are closed, and for a few moments there is profound stillness. Greenwood is here, being out on bail for the night. The effects of his long imprisonment are too evident in his wasted frame and pallid countenance; but his eye gleams with interest and tenderness as he looks around, forgetting all the sufferings of the past in the gladness of the occasion. With him are two younger brethren of the University of Cambridge, Francis Johnson and John Penry, matured in experience above their years. The choice of the church, expressed by their open suffrage, falls on Greenwood for the office of "doctor," or teacher. He is prevented by the restraints of imprisonment from taking the pastoral office and its active duties; but it is thought that he may instruct the church by his writings or by counsel even when in bonds. The brethren are not ashamed of his " chain "; they look upon it as " the mark in his body of the Lord Jesus."

It is expected that Francis Johnson, prior to his call, by the vote of the church, will give some account of his spiritual history and of his doctrinal views. The record of this confession is not before us, but from other sources of information we learn something of its outline.

" Brethren and companions in the faith and patience of our Lord Jesus. I greet you all in His blessed name. For a long time I was greatly opposed to this way. So much so, that when in Holland I went to the printing-office in Dort, at the instance of the English ambassador, to destroy the books written by our brethren, Henry Barrowe and John Greenwood. In my blind zeal against their cause, I destroyed all the copies, save two, one of which I gave to a friend, and the other I read to my own conviction. In obedience to that conviction, I come to you from Holland to acknowledge my brethren in bonds, and to cast in my lot amongst you."

Every heart is thrilled in listening to this simple statement, and to the declaration of faith given in addition. Johnson is chosen pastor.

The impression produced by Penry on the assembly, if possible, is still deeper. It is known that a price is set upon his head. For many months he sought shelter in the glens of Scotland; but, at the imperious demand of Queen Elizabeth, King James issued a decree forbidding any of his subjects to afford the fugitive either harbor or food on pain of death. Yet, knowing the wrath of the queen and the determination of the prelates to compass his death, he has journeyed from the extreme north of the island to London, in order to identify himself with this lowly band of confessors, now in the course of organization as a church of Christ. "I can accept no office amongst you, brethren, except to be the servant of all; for my purpose, if God shall give me opportunity, is to go before the queen, as with the halter round my neck, to plead that the gospel may be preached to my countrymen of Wales." The brethren do not press official distinction or responsibility on their devoted brother, after this touching avowal of his sacred determination. They are content to appoint Christopher Bowman and Nicolas Lee as deacons, with Daniel Studley and George Kniston as elders.

Seven infants are now presented by their parents for the ordinance of Christian baptism.

Brought as within the verge of heaven by these hallowed solemnities, and conscious of oneness in faith, in affection, and in purpose, they close the religious exercises of the evening by the administration of the Lord's Supper. How simple is the mode of preparation. A white cloth is spread upon the table. Five loaves are placed upon it, with the sacramental cup. The words of the institution, as given by our Lord Jesus on the night of the betrayal, are read. The pastor, with deep feeling, gives utterance to sentiments suited to the ordinance. The elements are distributed with becoming order, and a collection is made for the poor. Truly they sit together as "Christ's comrades," with the freedom of brethren, and yet with the reverence of disciples. In a low voice they sing the sacramental hymn, interrupted only by the overpowering emotions which constrain them to weep aloud in their solemn joy. To some of them it is the first and the last service of communion with the church on earth. They will meet the brethren after this manner no more, until they sit down at the marriage supper of the Lamb. Well may they linger; but the voice again is heard as in the Guest Chamber in Jerusalem, "Arise, let us go hence."

VI.

ARRESTED CHURCH-MEMBERS. — BARROW'S LETTER.

The proceedings of the newly-formed church, notwithstanding the caution exercised to keep them secret, did not long escape the attention of the authorities. John Greenwood, for a time, was suffered to lodge out of prison " within the rules," and, with Francis Johnson, he took up his abode at the house of Mr. Boyes, at Ludgate Hill. On the night of the 5th of December both of them were seized by the pursuivants, and thrown into "close prison." A few months afterward (March 4, 1592–3), the members of the church were surprised at a meeting, held on the spot where the Christians met during the Marian persecution, in the woods at Islington.

Fifty-six were taken prisoners, and sent, "two by two," to the jails of London, already crowded with the victims of intolerance. Silenced from preaching, they uttered remonstrances seldom exceeded in pathos or in force.

" Are we malefactors?" they demanded. " Are

we anywise undutiful to our prince? Maintain we any errors? Let us, then, be judicially convicted thereof, and delivered to the civil authority. We humbly pray, in the name of God and our sovereign the queen, that we may have the benefit of the laws and of the public charter of the land, namely, that we may be received to bail till we, by order of law, are convicted of some crime deserving of bonds. We plight unto your honors our faith unto God, and our allegiance to Her Majesty, that we will not commit any thing unworthy of the gospel of Christ, or to the disturbance of the common peace and good order of the land, and that we will be forthcoming at such reasonable warning as your Lordships shall command. Oh, let us not perish before trial and judgment, especially imploring and crying out to you for the same."

It was time to protest against the wrongs they endured. Sixteen had died in succession of the prison plague. Roger Rippon became the seventeenth victim. Others were sinking from want. Barrowe, for his companions in bonds, says: "Some of us had not one penny about us when we were sent to prison, nor any thing to procure a maintenance for ourselves and families, but our handy labor and trades, by which means not only we ourselves, but our families and children are undone and starved. That which we crave for us all is, the liberty to die openly, or live openly in the land of our nativity. If we deserve death, let us not be closely murdered, yea starved to death with hunger and cold, and stifled in loathsome dungeons."

These reiterated appeals were not altogether without effect. The bishops were compelled to give some show of legality to their proceedings by bringing the prisoners to open trial. To obtain evidence that might be adduced against them in court, they submitted the prisoners taken at Islington to personal inquisition. The report of these examinations is still preserved, and though the sufferers derived no relief at the time, it supplies facts for the vindication of their memory. Daniel Buck, a scrivener in Southwark, seems to have been one of the most communicative witnesses. " Being asked, what vow or promise he had made, when he came first into their society, he answered he made this protestation, that he would walk with the rest of the congregation as long as they did walk in the way of the Lord, and as far as might be warranted by the word of God. Being demanded, whether a motion had been made by some of their fraternity, that they should go somewhere into the country, whereby they might be in more safety,— denieth that he had heard of any such matter; but saith, he had heard one Miller (a preacher at St. Andrews Undershaft, Holborn) say, that if they did maintain the truth, they should not keep themselves in corners, but show themselves publicly, and defend the same; but he thought that unfit, lest it might be a means to stir a rebellion."

When the evidence of this kind had been collected, Barrowe, Greenwood, Saxio Bellot, gentleman, Daniel Studley, girdler, and Robert Bowle, fishmonger, were indicted at the sessions in Old Bailey, 21st of March, 1592–3, upon the Statute of 23 Eliz., for writing and publishing sundry seditious books and pamphlets, tending to the slander of the queen's government. Happily, for the sake of truth, we have, in a letter from Barrowe to a "certain countess of his kindred," an account of the proceedings. His statement is so necessary to a correct view of the case, that we give it entire.

" To the Right Honorable, etc. Though it be no new or strange doctrine unto you, Right Honorable and excellent Lady, who have been so educated and exercised in the faith and fear of God, that the cross should be joined to the gospel, tribulation and persecution to the faith and profession of Christ, yet may this seem strange unto you, and almost incredible, that, in a land professing Christ, such cruelty should be offered unto the servants of Christ for the truth and gospel's sake, and that by the chief ministers of the church, as they pretend.

" This no doubt doth make sundry, otherwise well affected, to think hardly of us and of our cause;

and specially, finding us by their instigation indicted, arraigned, and ready to be executed by the secular powers, for moving sedition and disobedience, for defaming the renowned person and government of our most gracious sovereign, Queen Elizabeth, and this state. But, right honorable, if our adversaries' proceedings, and our sufferings, with the true causes thereof, might be duly examined by the Scriptures, I doubt not but their malice and our innocency should easily appear to all men; however, now they think to cover the one and the other, by adding slander unto violence.

"Your Ladyship readeth, that the holy prophets, who spake in the name of God, yea, our blessed Saviour himself and his apostles, have suffered like usage, under the same pretence of sedition, innovation, rebellion against Cæsar and the state, at the hands and by the means of the chief ministers of that church, the priests, scribes, and Pharisees; men of no less account for holiness, learning, and authority than these our adversaries.

"The faithful of all ages since, that have witnessed against the malignant synagogue of antichrist, and stood for the gospel of Christ, have suffered like usage at the hands of the same prelacy and clergy that now is in the land, though possessed of other persons. The quarrel still remaineth betwixt the two opposite kingdoms of Christ and antichrist, and so long shall endure as any part of the apostasy and usurped tyranny of the man of sin shall remain. The apostasy and tyranny of antichrist, as it sprung not at once or in a day, but by degrees wrought from his mystery to his manifestation and exaltation in his throne, so was he not at once wholly discovered or abolished; but as Christ, from time to time, by the beams of his appearing, discovered the iniquity, so by the power of his word, which cannot be made of none effect, doth he abolish the same; and shall not cease this war until antichrist, with his army, power, and ministry, be wholly cast out of the church. Assurance and manifest revelation hereof we have, both in general and particular, in that historical prophecy given of Christ unto his church by John the divine, in the book of the Revelation, from the tenth to the twentieth chapter; proof and accomplishment hereof, we have hitherto found in the abolishing of all the errors, idolatries, trumperies, and forgeries discovered and witnessed against by the faithful servants of Christ in former ages. Neither is there cause why we should doubt of the like sequel and event in the present and future times, seeing the enormities remaining are no less hateful to God, and contrary to the kingdom of Christ; and God, that condemneth them, is a strong God to execute his will, which no opposition or tyranny of his adversaries shall be able to hinder or resist.

"Whiles then we be, in the mercy of God, holding the most holy and glorious cause of Christ against them, that he might reign in his church by such officers and laws as he hath prescribed in his testament, we fear not our adversaries in any thing, knowing that their malice and opposition herein is made to them a token of perdition, and to us of salvation, and that of God. For this we are bold, both to stand for the holy ministry, government, and ordinances of Christ prescribed in his word, and also to withstand and witness against this antichristian hierarchy of the prelacy and clergy of this land, in their ministry, ministration, government, courts, officers, canons, etc., which I, by writing, have showed to have no ground or warrant in God's word; not to be given, or to belong unto the church of Christ, but to be invented by man; the very same that the pope still useth, and erewhile used and left in this land, the like others of us more learned have offered, and do still offer, upon the dispense of our lives, and to prove by the express word of God, in any Christian and peaceable conference, against any whosoever that will there stand for the defence of the same.

"The prelates, seeing the axe thus laid to the root of the tree of their pomp, not able to prove their ministry, ministration, and government which they usurp and exercise in the church by the Scriptures, sought to turn away this question, and to get rid of their adversaries, by other subtle and hostile practices, as at the first, by shutting up the chief of us in their close prisons; by defaming us in their pulpits, printed books, and sparsed libels in the land; by seeking to inveigle us with certain subtle questions to bring our lives into danger; by suborned conferences with certain of their select instruments; not to speak of their manifold molestations and cruel usage at their commandment showed us in the prisons. To their reproachful and slanderous books, being set of God, though most unworthy, and suffering for the defence of the faith, and being thus provoked by them, I held it my duty, according to the small measure of grace received, to make answer, which I also did more than three years since. Likewise, to deliver ourselves from the false report and witness that might be made against us in those conferences, we thought good to publish them to the land. For these books, written more than three years since, after well near six years' imprisonment sustained at their hands, have these prelates, by their vehement suggestions and accusations, caused us to be now indicted, arraigned, and condemned for writing and publishing seditious books, upon the same statute made the 23d year of Her Majesty's reign. Their accusations were drawn into these heads:

"*First.* That I should write and publish the Queen's Majesty to be unbaptized.

"*Secondly.* The state to be wholly corrupted from the crown of the head to the sole of the foot, in the laws, judgments, judges, customs, etc., so that none that feared God could live in peace therein.

"*Thirdly.* That all the people in the land are infidels.

"To these indictments I answered generally, that either they were mistaken, or else misconstrued; neither in my meaning, matter, or words, any such crime could justly be found; my meaning being just, and without evil toward any man, much more toward my sovereign and the state, whom I from the heart honored. The matters, being merely ecclesiastical, controverted betwixt the clergy and us; my words being either in answer of their slanders, or in assertion of such things as I hold; that if I had offended in any of my words, it was rather casual through haste, than of any evil intent.

"More particularly to the first, concerning the queen's baptism, I answered, that it was utterly mistaken, both contrary to my meaning and to my express words in that place of my book, as manifestly appeareth to any indifferent reader.

"That I there purposely defended Her Majesty's baptism received, against such as hold the baptism given in popery to be no baptism at all; where I proved that it needed not to be repeated; yet there I also showed such baptism, given in popery, not to seal God's covenant to the church in that estate; and therefore that the abuse ought, by all that had there received it, to be repented.

"To the second indictment, I showed the words by me used to be drawn from Isaiah i. and Rev. xiii., that I had no evil mind toward the state, laws, or judges, but only showed that when the ministry, the salt, the light is corrupted, the body and all the parts must needs be unsound, which I immediately, in the same place of that book, showed by the general breach of the laws of both Tables, by all estates, degrees, persons, etc., setting down the particulars.

"To the third indictment, I answered, that I gladly embraced and believed the common faith received and professed in this land, as most holy and sound; that I had reverend estimation of sundry, and good hope of many thousands in the land; though I utterly disliked the present constitution of this church, in the present communion, ministry, ministration, worship, government, and ordinances ecclesiastical of these cathedral and parishional assemblies.

"Some other few things such as they thought might most make against us, were culled out of my writings, and urged, as that I should hold Her Majesty to be antichristian, and her government antichristian.

"To which I answered, that it was with great and manifest injury so collected; seeing in sundry places of that book, and everywhere in all my writings and sayings, I have protested my exceeding good opinion and reverend estimation of Her Majesty's royal person and government, above all other princes in the world, for her most rare and singular virtues and endowments. I have everywhere in my writings acknowledged all duty and obedience to Her Majesty's government, as to the sacred ordinance of God, the supreme power he hath set over all causes and persons, whether ecclesiastical or civil, within her dominions; always desiring to be intended (understood) of this false ecclesiastical government, foreign power, canons, and courts, brought in and usurped by the prelates and their accomplices.

"But these answers, or whatsoever else I could say or allege, prevailed nothing; all things being so hardly construed and urged against me (no doubt through the prelates' former instigations and malicious accusations). So that I, with my four other brethren, were the 23d of the third month (1592–3) condemned and adjudged to suffer death as felons, upon these indictments aforesaid. Upon the 24th, early in the morning, was preparation made for our execution; we brought out of the limbo, our irons smitten off, and we ready to be bound to the cart, when Her Majesty's most gracious pardon came for our reprieve.

"After that, the bishops sent unto us certain doctors and deans to exhort and confer with us. We showed how they had neglected the time; we had been wellnigh six years in their prisons; never refused, but always humbly desired of them Christian conference, for the peaceable discussing and deciding our differences, but could never obtain it at their hands; neither did these men, all this time, come unto us, or offer any such matter; that our time was short in this world, neither were we to bestow it unto controversies, so much as unto more profitable and comfortable considerations; yet, if they desired to have conference with us, they were to get our lives respited thereunto; then, if they would join unto us two other of our brethren in their prisons, whom we named unto them, we then gladly would condescend to any Christian and orderly conference, by the Scriptures, with such or so many of them as should be thought meet.

"Upon the last day of the third month, my brother Greenwood and I were very early and secretly conveyed to the place of execution; where, being tied by the necks to the tree, we were permitted to speak a few words. We there, in the sight of that Judge that knoweth and searcheth the heart, before whom we were then immediately to appear, protested our loyalty and innocency toward Her Majesty, our nobles, governors, magistrates, and this whole state;

that in our writings we had no malicious or evil intent, so much as in thought, toward any of these, or toward any person in the world; that wherein we had through zeal, or unadvisedly, let fall any word or sentence that moved offence, or carried any show of irreverence, we were heartily sorry, and humbly besought pardon of them so offended for the same. Further, we exhorted the people to obedience and hearty love of their prince and magistrates, to lay down their lives in their defence against all enemies; yea, at their hands meekly and patiently to receive death, or any punishment they shall inflict, whether justly or unjustly. We exhorted them, also, unto orderly, quiet, and peaceable walking within the limits of their own calling, to the holy fear and true worship of God.

"For the books written by us, we exhorted all men no further to receive any thing therein contained, than they should find sound proof of the same in the Holy Scriptures. Thus craving pardon of all men whom we had any way offended, and freely forgiving the whole world, we used prayer for Her Majesty, the magistrates, people, and even for our adversaries; and having both of us almost finished our last words, behold one was even at that instant come with a reprieve for our lives from Her Majesty, which was not only thankfully received of us, but with exceeding rejoicing and applause of all the people, both at the place of execution, and in the way, streets, and houses as we returned.

"Thus pleased it God to dispose the utmost violence of our adversaries, to the manifestation of our innocency, concerning the crimes whereof we were accused and condemned; and not only so, but also to the further showing forth of Her Majesty's princely clemency, rare virtue, and Christian care of her faithful subjects, to the yet further manifesting of her renowned fame and love amongst all her people. And sure we have no doubt but the same, our gracious God, that hath wrought this marvellous work in Her Majesty's princely heart, to cause of her own accord and singular wisdom, even before she knew our innocency, twice to stay the execution of that rigorous sentence, will now much more, after so assured and wonderful demonstration of our innocency, move Her gracious Majesty freely and fully to pardon (prevent) the execution thereof, as she that never desired, and always loathly shed the blood of her greatest enemies, much less will she now of her loyal Christian and innocent subjects; especially if Her Majesty might be truly informed, both of the things that are passed, and of our lamentable estate and great misery wherein we now continue in a miserable place and case, in the loathsome jail of Newgate, under this heavy judgment, every day expecting execution.

"Hereunto if God shall move your noble heart, right virtuous lady, not for any worldly cause (which for my present reproach and baseness I dare not mention to your honor), so much as for the love and cause of Christ which we, through the grace of God, profess; to inform Her Majesty of our entire faith unto God, unstained loyalty to Her Highness, innocency and good conscience toward all men; in pardoning our offence and judgment, or else in removing our poor worn bodies out of this miserable jail (the horror whereof is not to be spoken unto your honor), to some more honest and meet place, if she vouchsafe us longer to live. Your Ladyship doubtless shall herein do a right Christian and gracious act, acceptable to God, behooveful to your sovereign prince, comfortable to us the poor condemned prisoners of Christ, yea, to his whole afflicted church, and, most of all, to your own praise and comfort in this life and in the life to come. Hereunto further to exhort your honor, by the examples of the godly of like condition, in such times of public distresses and danger, I hope I need not so much as to stir up that good gift and grace of God which is in you, not to neglect or put from you this notable occasion sent unto you from God, to show forth the naturalness of your faith unto Him, of your fidelity to your prince, of your love to the members of Christ in distress, whom as you succor or neglect herein, so assure yourself will Christ in His glory esteem it as done, or denied to be done, by you to His own sacred person.

"Let not, therefore, right dear and elect lady, any worldly or politic impediments or unlikelihoods, no fleshly fears, diffidence or delays, stop or hinder you from speaking to Her Majesty on our behalf, before she go out of this city, lest we, by your default herein, perish in her absence, having no assured stay or respite of our lives; and our malignant adversaries ready to watch any occasion for the shedding of our blood, as we see by those two near and miraculous escapes have found.

"Only, good Madam, do your diligent endeavor herein, and counsel the success, as we also with you shall, unto God in our prayers; which, howsoever it fall out, magnified be the blessed name of God in these our mortal bodies, whether by life or death. His mighty hand that hath hitherto upholden us, assist us to the finishing up this last part of our warfare to the vanquishing of our last enemy, death, with all his terrors, and to the attaining of that crown of glory which is purchased for us in the blood of Christ, laid up and truly kept for us in the hand of God; and not only for us, but for all that keep the faith and commandments of Jesus. Of which number, noble lady, I hear and hope you are; and shall not cease (God willing) whiles I here live, to further the same unto you by my prayers and utmost endeavors. His grace and blessing, the prayers of the saints, and mine unworthy service be with you. This 4th or 5th of the fourth month, 1593.

"Your honor's humbly, at commandment, during life, condemned of men, but received of God.

"HENRY BARROWE."

We are not able to identify in the court of Elizabeth, the "Countess" to whom Barrowe made this touching and solemn appeal, nor can we learn what steps were taken to prevent the execution. From a private letter we find that Lord Burghley interfered to secure a reprieve. He submitted to the archbishop a proposition for peace from Barrowe in the following terms: "My humble desire is to you and any that fear God, and even to my greatest adversaries in these ecclesiastical controversies, or (I hope) our brotherly differences, if we may come to Christian and peaceful conference with some learned and moderate persons, where the reasons on each side may be with deliberation set down and expounded by the word of God, and so His truth therein appearing may be embraced, and we brought to unity in the truth, and these wounds which now are made, and likely to shed even streams of blood, may be healed. Those faithful of our mind which yet remain, and such as God, no doubt, will raise up in this cause of Christ may be reunited. Yea, when all of us may be united in Christ, our head, with joy. And howsoever it shall please God and Her excellent Majesty to dispose of our lives, yet we hereby being brought to the sight of such faults as we are charged to have committed (but yet see not), may then humbly acknowledge the same, and suffer such punishments as are inflicted to the good example of others, to the honor of Her Majesty and her state, and thus, as in the sight of Christ, I vow, by His grace, and dare assure, on the behalf of my Christian brethren like minded, that you, or any of you, taking this Christian and brotherly pains, shall reason and prove us by every word of God to agree with you and be obedient unto His whole will." This proposal met with no favor from the Episcopal bench. The Archbishop of Canterbury "was very peremptory, so as the Lord Treasurer gave him and the Bishop of Worcester some round taxing words, and used some speech to the queen, but was not seconded by any, which hath made him remiss as is thought." *

The object sought by the bishops was unconditional submission. A recantation, however insincere, would have saved the lives of the prisoners. The attorney-general wrote to the Lord Keeper in the case as follows:

* State Paper MSS. Letter of Thos. Phillips.

" My most humble duty to your Lordship, —

" This day, by virtue of the last commission of oyer and terminer in London, the court hath proceeded against Barrowe and Greenwood for devising, and against Scipio Bellott, Robert Bowle, and Daniel Studley, for publishing and dispersing seditious books; and they are all attainted by verdict and judgment, and direction given for execution to be done to-morrow as in case of like quality.

" None showed any token of recognition of their offence and prayer of mercy for the same, saving Bellott alone, who desireth conference, and to be reformed of his errors, and with tears affirmeth himself to be sorry that he hath been misled.

" The others pretend loyalty and obedience to Her Majesty, and endeavor to draw all that they have most maliciously written and published against Her Majesty's government, to the bishops and ministers of the church only, and as not meant against her highness; which being most evident against them, and so found by the jury, yet not one of them made any countenance of submission; but rather persisted in that they be convicted of. This I have thought good to make known to your Lordship; to the end, that if Her Majesty's pleasure should be to have execution deferred, it might be known this night, and order given accordingly; otherwise, the direction given by the judges in open court will prevail; and so I commit your Lordship to the Almighty. 23 Martii, 1592—3.

" Your Lordship's most humble at commandment.
" THO. EGERTON."

Three days after, " Mr. Attorney " writes: " I have spent this whole afternoon at a fruitless, idle conference, and am but now returned, both weary and weak. If my health will serve me, I will wait upon your Lordships to-morrow morning, and make report of the day's exercise. I have sent to your Lordships, here enclosed, an act of the bill in the lower house against recusants, reformed as the committee have brought it again into the house. How it is in any thing changed in substance from the title, as it was first exhibited, doth appear in the marginal notes, which, to-morrow, I will more fully declare to your Lordships, if it shall please your honor to give me leave. And rest in all things at your Lordships' commandment, the 26th of March, 1593.

" Your Lordships' most humble at commandment.
" THO. EGERTON."

The change made in the "bill," to which the attorney-general refers, appears to have decided the fate of Barrowe and Greenwood. Phillips, in a letter to his "loving friend," Mr. William Sterrell, gives curious particulars on the subject. He says:

"There was a bill preferred against the Barrowists and Brownists, making it felony to maintain any opinions against the ecclesiastical government, which, by the bishops' means, did pass the upper house, but was found so captious by the nether house as it was thought it would never have passed in any sort, for it was thought all the Puritans would have been drawn within the compass thereof. Yet, by the earnest laboring of those (who) sought to satisfy the bishops' humors, it is passed to this effect, that whosoever shall be an obstinant recusant, refusing to come to any church, and do deny the Queen to have any power or authority in ecclesiastical causes, and do by writing or otherwise publish the same, and be a keeper of conventicles also, being convicted, he shall abjure the realm within three months, and lose all his goods and lands; if he return without leave, it shall be felony. Thus have they minced it, as is thought, so as it will not reach to any man, that shall deserve favor, in a concurrence of so many faults and actions. The week before, upon the late conventicle you wrote of last, Barrowe and Greenwood, with some others, were indicted, arraigned, and condemned, upon the statute of writing and publishing seditious books, and would have been executed, but, as they were ready to be braced up, were reprieved; but, the day after the court house (the House of Lords) had showed their dislike of this bill, were early in the morning hanged. It is plainly said that their execution proceeded of malice of the bishops, to spite the nether house, which hath procured them much hatred among the common people affected that way." *

This remarkable document, dated April 7, 1593, was written the day after the execution of Barrowe and Greenwood, and supplies, in consequence, the most authentic evidence as to the instigators of their death.

It is said that the Queen was somewhat moved on hearing of the event. She asked Dr. Reynolds what he thought of Mr. Barrowe and Mr. Greenwood. He answered Her Majesty that it could not avail any thing to show his judgment concerning them, seeing they were put to death; and, being unwilling to speak his mind further, the Queen charged him upon his allegiance to speak. He replied, " that he was persuaded, if they had lived, they would have been two as worthy instruments for the church of God as have been raised up in their age." Her Majesty sighed, and said no more. On a subsequent occasion, the Queen riding in a park, near the place of execution, inquired of the Earl of Cumberland, who was present when they suffered, what end they made. He answered, " A very godly end, and prayed for your Majesty and the state,

* State Paper MSS.

etc." Finally, the Queen asked the archbishop what he thought of Barrowe and Greenwood, in his conscience. In reply, he said he thought they were servants of God, but dangerous to the state. "Alas!" rejoined the Queen, "shall we put the servants of God to death?"

VII.

PENRY, THE PILGRIM MARTYR.

On the day of the martyrdom of Barrowe and Greenwood, their brother and companion, John Penry, wrote an affecting letter from prison to his wife, in which he gives the particulars of his apprehension on the 22d of the preceding month.

"I see my blood laid for," he says, " (my beloved), and so my days and testimony drawing to an end (for aught I know), and, therefore, I think it my duty to leave behind me this testimony of my love to so dear a sister, and so loving a wife in the Lord as you have been to me. . . . If the Lord shall end my days in this testimony, as blessed be His name, howsoever it may be, I am ready and content with His good pleasure. Keep yourself, my good Helen, here with this poor church. You may make all good refuge, and stay here, as any widow else, for your outward estate. Though you could not, yet I know that you had rather dwell under the wings of the God of Israel in poverty, with godly

Ruth, than to possess kingdoms in the land of Moab; and what shift soever you make, keep our poor children with you, that you may bring them up yourself in the instruction and information of the Lord. I leave you and them, indeed, nothing in this life, but the blessing of my God; and His blessed promises, made unto me a poor wretched sinner, that my seed, my habitation, and family should be blessed and happy upon the earth; and thus, my sister, I doubt not shall be found an ample portion both for you and them; though you know that in hunger often, in cold often, in poverty and nakedness, we must make account to profess the gospel in this life. . . . I know, my good Helen, that the burden which I lay upon thee of four infants, whereof the eldest is not four years old, will not seem in any way burdensome to thee. . . . Salute the whole church from me, especially those in bonds, and be you all much and heartily saluted. Let none of them be dismayed; the Lord will send a glorious issue unto your troubles. Yet, you must all be prepared for sufferings, I see likelihood. Let not those which are abroad miss to frequent their holy meetings."

The entire correspondence of Penry,* at this trying period, affords a subject for the most interesting study.

* See "Penry, the Pilgrim Martyr," published by the Cong. Board of Publication.

For more than two centuries his name has been branded with infamy, and writers of ecclesiastical history, so called, have represented him as a vile and reckless incendiary, without principle, and detestable for his spirit and practices. We find, however, from the affecting prison letters addressed to his family and to his brethren of the church, a combination of integrity, wisdom, and tenderness, seldom met with under circumstances so likely to test the character and disposition.

Penry was true to his principles and to the cause he had firmly espoused. He remained, therefore, inflexible in his adherence to the views he had broached as the result of deep and settled conviction. But in his course we have a striking example to show the compatibility of the sternest rectitude with the finest sensibility. The heart of the husband and of the father is laid open to us, whilst we see in him, at the same time, the courage of the champion, the zeal of an apostle, and the patience of the martyr. He was not indifferent to life. On the contrary, he had the strongest reasons, arising from the ties of affection, to desire its preservation. He made every effort, consistent with regard to the interests of truth, to arrest the fatal stroke intended against him; and he urged his beloved and devoted wife to take their four helpless children to the judges to move them to compassion. The attempt was vain. She might as well have tried to move a rock or to melt an iceberg. The practical answer given by one of the ermined savages to her appeal, was to commit a Christian widow, who accompanied her, to prison, simply on suspicion of complicity with the Separatists, from the fact of her association with the wife of Penry. But, for a moment, throughout this perplexing and heart-rending experience, the martyr never lost sight of the moral grandeur of the cause for which he suffered.

"If my blood," he said, "were an ocean sea, and every drop were a life unto me, I would give them all, by the help of the Lord, for the maintenance of the same, my confession. Yet if any error can be shown therein, that I will not maintain." To the last he evinced the utmost calmness, strengthening and comforting others, and indicating to them the course of Christian duty. In reading the following passages from his letter to the church, we must bear in mind the wretchedness of his outward condition. Torn from his family, at the age of thirty-four, with all his warm and gushing affections; denied the sight of his wife, and refused all opportunity to embrace, for the last time, children he loved so tenderly; left in a gloomy cell, with no place for rest except on a filthy litter; watched incessantly by the authorities to prevent, if possible, all communication with his friends, and brought up, at the pleasure of the justices, to answer questions to his own injury, or to listen to their bitter taunts and reproaches, he yet found means to communicate his thoughts in terms the most eloquent and impressive, and in a tone of almost supernatural calmness.

"Beloved!" he writes, "let us think our lot and portion more than blessed, that are now vouchsafed the favor, not only to know and to profess, but also to suffer for the sincerity of the gospel; and let us remember that great is our reward in Heaven, if we endure unto the end.

"I testify unto you, for mine own part, as I shall answer before Jesus Christ and his elect angels, that I never saw any truth more clear and undoubted than this witness wherein we stand. . . . And I thank my God I am not only ready to be bound and banished, but even to die in this cause by His strength. Yea, my brethren, I greatly long, in regard of myself, to be dissolved, and to live in the blessed kingdom of heaven with Jesus Christ and his angels; with Adam, Enoch, Noah, Abraham, Moses, Job, David, Jeremy, Daniel, Paul, the great Apostle of the Gentiles; and with the rest of the holy saints, both men and women; with the glorious kings, prophets, and martyrs, and witnesses of Jesus Christ, that have been from the beginning of the world; particularly with my two dear brethren, Master Henry Barrowe and Master John Greenwood, which have, last of all, yielded their blood for this precious testimony. Confessing unto you, my brethren and sisters, that if I might live upon this earth the days of Methuselah twice told, and that in no less comfort than Peter, James, and John were in the Mount; and, after this life, might be sure of the kingdom of heaven; that yet, to gain all this, I durst not go from the former testimony. Wherefore, my brethren, I beseech you to be of like mind herein with me. . . .

" Strive for me and with me, that the Lord our God may make me and us all able to end our course with joy and patience. . . .

" I would, indeed, if it be His good pleasure, live yet with you, to help you to bear that grievous and hard yoke which yet ye are like to sustain, either here or in a strange land.

" And, my good brethren, seeing banishment with loss of goods is likely to betide you all, prepare yourselves for this hard entreaty, and rejoice that you are made worthy, for Christ's cause, to suffer and bear all these things. And I beseech you, in the bowels of Jesus Christ, that none of you in this case look upon his particular estate, but regard the general state of the church of God; that the same may go and be kept together whithersoever it shall please God to send you. Oh! the blessing will be great that shall ensue this care. Whereas if you go, every man to provide for his own house, and to look for his own family, first neglecting poor Zion, the Lord will set his face against you, and scatter you from the one end of heaven to the other; neither shall you find a resting-place for the soles of your feet, or a blessing upon any thing you take in hand. . . .

"Let not those of you, then, that either have stocks in your hands, or some likely trades to live by, dispose of yourselves where it may be most commodious for your outward estate, and in the mean time suffer the poor ones, that have no such means, either to bear the whole work upon their weak shoulders, or to end their days in sorrow and mourning for want of outward and inward comforts in the land of strangers; for the Lord will be an avenger of all such dealings. But consult with the whole church, yea, with the brethren of other places, how the church may be kept together and built, whithersoever they go. Let not the poor and the friendless be forced to stay behind here, and to break a good conscience for want of your support and kindness unto them, that they may go with you.

"And here, I humbly beseech you, not in any outward regard, as I shall answer before my God, that you would take my poor and desolate widow, and my mess of fatherless and friendless orphans with you into exile, whithersoever you go; and you shall find, I doubt not, that the blessed promises of my God, made unto me and mine, will accompany them, and even the whole church for their sakes. . . .

"Be kind, loving, and tender-hearted, the one of you toward the other; labor every way to increase love, and to show the duties of love, one of you toward another, by visiting, comforting, and relieving one the other, even for the reproach of the heathen that are round about us (as the Lord saith). Be watching in prayer; especially remember those of our brethren that are especially endangered; particularly those our two brethren, Mr. Studley and Robert Bowl, whom our God hath strengthened now to stand in the fore-front of the battle.

"I fear me, that our carelessness was over great to sue unto God for the lives of those two so notable lights of His church, who now rest with Him, and that He took them away for many respects seeming good to His wisdom; so, also, that we might be careful in prayer in all such causes. . . . Pray for the brethren, and for our brother, Mr. Francis Johnson; and for me, who am likely to end my days either with them or before them, that our God may spare us unto His church, if it be His good pleasure, or give us exceeding faithfulness; and be every way comfortable unto the sister and wife of the dead, I mean my beloved M. Barrowe and M.

Greenwood, whom I most heartily salute, and desire much to be comforted in their God, who, by His blessings from above, will countervail unto them the want of so notable a brother and husband."

In the deep obscurity that rests upon all the movements of the church, struggling for existence against such formidable opposition, we cannot determine, with certainty, how far its influence extended. But the request of Penry, that the brethren would communicate with those who held the same faith in different parts of the country shows that the church in London was not a solitary community. Considered in anticipation of the subsequent movement of the Pilgrim Fathers to America, the words of the martyr have a significance semi-prophetic:

"I would wish you earnestly to write; yea, to send, if you may, to comfort the brethren in the west and north countries, that they faint not in these troubles, and that also you may have of their advice, and they of yours, what to do in these desolate times; and, if you think of any thing for their comfort and direction, send them conveniently a copy of this my letter, and of the Declaration of faith and allegiance, wishing them, before whomsoever they be called, that their own mouths be not had in witness against them in any thing; yea, I would wish you and them to be together, if you may, whithersoever you shall be banished; and to this purpose, to bethink you beforehand where to be; yea, to send some who may be meet to prepare you some resting-place; and be all of you assured that He, who is your God in England, will be your God in any land under the whole heaven; for the earth and the fulness thereof are His, and blessed are they that, for his cause, are bereaved of any part of the same."

From a petition of the church, to which we shall shortly refer, Penry and his friends must have directed their thoughts to the western hemisphere. With his dying hand, from the gallows in Southwark, he pointed to the future home of the Pilgrims, a country at this day numbering a population of thirty millions.*

The brethren, to whom Penry addressed his touching appeal, were not wanting in effort to save the lives of the brethren "specially endangered." They petitioned the Queen, and sent a memorial to the Privy Council, the Lord Mayor, and the magistrates of the city, but without success. On the 25th of May, after a mock trial, the fatal sentence was pro-

---

* Impressed with this sublime incident, the writer of these lines, with the members of the Pilgrim Church in Southwark, erected a corner-stone of a memorial building on the 29th of May, 1856, inscribed with the name of Penry. There it has remained four years, a fragment with the appearance of a ruin, waiting until the sons of the Pilgrims shall complete it as a *Pillar of Witness*.

nounced. Archbishop Whitgift was the first to sign his death-warrant, with Sir John Popham and others. The friends of Penry anticipated that he would be led forth to die after the expiration of the usual term allowed after the verdict. A concourse, numerous and orderly as that collected to witness the execution of Barrowe and Greenwood, would no doubt have accompanied Penry to manifest their sympathy; but, to prevent such a demonstration, the sheriff was directed to surprise the prisoner a day or two before. On the 29th of May, Penry was suddenly ordered, when at dinner, to prepare for death in the afternoon at four o'clock. He was led, at five, from the prison in High Street borough, to the gallows erected at St. Thomas, a watering in the Old Kent road, Southwark. A small company of persons, seeing the workmen making preparations, had collected together. Penry would have spoken, but the sheriff insisted that neither in protestation of his loyalty, nor in the avowal of his innocence, should he utter a word. His life was taken, and the people were dispersed. The place of his burial is unknown. But

> "Though nameless, trampled, and forgot,
> His servant's humble ashes lie;
> God has marked and sealed the spot,
> To call its inmate to the sky."

VIII.

FIRST PLANS FOR MIGRATING TO NEW ENGLAND.

The mariners of England directed great attention to the Western Hemisphere in the reign of Elizabeth; Raleigh, Frobisher, Drake, Gilbert, Lane, Hariot, and Cavendish, sought in succession to secure a settlement in America.

Sir Walter Raleigh, in particular, was bent on this object. Often defeated in plans, and unjustly treated, he returned to it with ardor and resolution whenever an opportunity arose to put forth fresh effort. He had received his military training in connection with the Huguenots of France, and the massacre of the colony sent by them to Florida made a strong impression upon his mind.

Some of the miserable men, who had escaped the furious carnage of the Spaniards, found their way to England, and received aid and encouragement from Raleigh. They were introduced at court, and from that period public interest was awakened in the subject of colonization in America. In the first instance,

Raleigh preferred to form a plantation north of Virginia; "for the apparent danger," says Captain Smith, "all the colonies may be in if this be not possessed by the English, to prevent the Spaniard who already hath seated himself on the north of Florida and on the back of Virginia, where he is already possessed of rich silver mines, and will no doubt vomit his fury and malice upon the neighbor plantations, if a prehabitation do not anticipate his intentions."

The melancholy fate of the colonists at Roanoke is well known to the student of American history. Enchanted by the descriptions, given by Philip Amidas and Arthur Barlow, of the delightful region, the fragrance of which was like that of "some delicate garden, abounding with all kinds of odoriferous flowers," a company of emigrants sailed from Plymouth for this transatlantic paradise in 1585. The expedition consisted of seven vessels, and carried one hundred and eight colonists to the shores of Carolina, accompanied by men of science and commanders of great nautical experience. Manteo, one of the natives who returned with the fleet from a visit to England, was sent ashore to announce their arrival. Their reception by the aborigines was favorable, and, with ordinary prudence, they might have gained their confidence. But they were wanting in prudence and in just consideration of others.

For an act of theft by the Indians, Grenville, the English commander, ordered the village to be burnt and the standing corn to be destroyed.

After the return of the fleet, the colonists explored the country, and reported its wonderful beauty and fertility. They spoke in contemptuous terms of the natives as too feeble to inspire terror.

Mad with the passion for gold, the new settlers pushed their way into the country with no regard to the proper means of safety. One of the Indian chiefs, unsuspecting danger, was lured by them into a kind of ambush, and put to death with his principal followers.

Wearied after a time with their enterprise, and impatient for supplies, which were on the way, the colonists seized the first opportunity to return to England. They came home, in the fleet of Sir Francis Drake, to disparage the country with which they had expressed themselves so charmed and satisfied.

Sir Richard Grenville, on his arrival only a fortnight after with stores for the infant settlement, found it completely deserted. Unwilling that the post should be entirely abandoned, he left fifteen men as a garrison on the Island of Roanoke.

A second company of settlers, with wives and families, were sent out by Raleigh in 1587. They found the fort in ruins, and around it the bleached bones of their countrymen who had been murdered by the Indians. Disasters thickened upon them. Alarmed and anxious, the colonists urged John White, their governor, to return to England for reinforcements and supplies. He left eighty-nine men, seventeen women, and two children in the "city of Raleigh," expecting to enlist the sympathies of their friends in the mother country on their behalf. His daughter and granddaughter remained behind in the settlement, as hostages, to satisfy the colonists that all his energies would be devoted, when absent from them, to their interests.

Unhappily White, on reaching the mother country, could not secure relief in time to save the colony. The threatened invasion of Spain absorbed the attention of all classes. Raleigh, indeed, found means to despatch White with supplies in two vessels. But instead of pursuing a direct course, they tried to seize prizes of war, and suffered, in consequence, in an engagement at sea. They were disabled in the conflict, and were compelled to return to England. In the meanwhile, the poor colonists at Roanoke perished without leaving a vestige to trace their existence. In 1590, White returned to search for his daughter and the settlers, but without success.

This rapid sketch of the course of things, in reference to colonization, is needful to understand the terms of a petition presented about this time by the Separatists, after the martyrdom of Barrowe, Greenwood, and Penry. If men were still wanted, as a forlorn hope in those distant regions, they were prepared, trusting in God to venture into the breach.

If England needed to have a frontier line of firm and all-enduring colonists to break the force of a Spanish irruption, and to screen other settlers who might otherwise be exposed, they offered their services for such a purpose. They were influenced by no mercenary motive, nor were they consumed by the thirst for gold. The only satisfaction they sought was that arising from freedom of religious worship. The fact that they could not attach their names to a petition for the object, without peril from the authorities, only enhances its moral interest. These remarks will prepare the reader to regard with peculiar interest the following document. "The humble petition of Her Highness' faithful subjects, falsely called Brownists. To the Right Honorable the Lords of Her Majesty's most honorable privy council:

"Whereas we, Her Majesty's natural born subjects, true and loyal, now lying many of us in other countries as men exiled Her Majesty's dominions, and the rest which remain within Her Grace's land, greatly distressed through imprisonment and other great troubles sustained only for some matters of conscience, in which our most lamentable estate we cannot, in that measure, perform the duty of subjects as we desire. And, also, whereas means are now offered for our being in a foreign and far country, which lieth to the west from hence in the province of Canada,* where, by the Providence of the Almighty and Her Majesty's most gracious favor, we may not only worship God, as we are in conscience persuaded by His word, but also do unto Her Majesty and our country great good service, and in time also greatly annoy that bloody and persecuting Spaniard about the Bay of Mexico. Our most humble suit is, that it may please your Honors to be a means unto her Excellent Majesty, that with Her Majesty's most gracious favor and protection, we may peaceably depart thither, and there remaining to be accounted Her Majesty's faithful and loving subjects, to whom we owe all duty and obedience in the Lord. Promising hereby, and taking God to record, who searcheth the hearts of all people, that wheresoever we be come, we will, by the grace of God, love and die faithful to Her Highness and this land of our nativity."

---

* The name Canada was given to an extensive territory, including what was subsequently called New England. In Francis de Creux's Historia Canadensis a map is given of 1660, in which Newfoundland, Nova Scotia, and New England, are included in Canada, extending to Michigan and Lake Superior.

The ideas of the petitioners, to modern readers, must appear extremely confused. "Canada" and the "Bay of Mexico," as we now understand the subject, are too widely apart to be comprehended in the same description. But there can be no doubt as to the purpose of these heroic men, in relation to the interests of their country and the counteracting influence to be exerted on the cruel Spaniards. What if the Pilgrims of 1620 had been anticipated by the companions of the martyrs in 1593? What if the principles of the Plymouth Colony had leavened the South as they formed the men of the North? It was not so ordered. The Lords of the Privy Council would not deign to give a reply to the petitioners. They wanted pioneers in the New World, men with inward resources sufficient to make themselves at home in the wilderness. But they could not reconcile themselves to the thought that "Brownists" might be permitted to breathe freely, though three thousand miles away.

It was necessary that further experiments should be made in colonization, to exhaust the wisdom and the resources of the mighty and of the noble, before the promoters of the schemes for "plantation" would condescend to accept the people fitted in Providence for the work.

IX.

MORE IMPRISONMENTS.—FRANCIS JOHNSON.

How the Christians in bonds found means to write amidst the confusion of the common prison on the one hand, and the incessant vigilance of the keeper on the other, remains to us a mystery. Penry, in a letter to his wife, says: " I got means, this day, to write this much, whereof no creature living knoweth." In a long and deeply affecting communication intended for his daughters, and to be read by them when they should come to years of discretion, he tells them: " I have written this in that scarcity of paper, ink, and time, that I could do it no otherwise than first it came into my mind, and set it down."

In the original manuscripts there are few indications of haste. The writing is even, often neat, and, in the margin, Scripture references are marked with striking exactness. Did they secrete materials for correspondence supplied to them stealthily by friends? Did they watch for the first rays of the morning, and record their thoughts when the motley crowd of fellow prisoners were fast aleep? We cannot tell. But, as we take into the hand the papers moistened with their tears, we are thankful that the precious fragments remain.

The communications of Francis Johnson, speaking comparatively, are rather extensive. Left in the Clink prison, after the martyrdom of his brethren, he wrote to Lord Burghley, enclosing a petition to the Queen. " Many," he says, "know not our cause, and either speak evil of that they know not, or at least offer us not any way to help us, if they do not also seek, by all means, to add to our afflictions. Of them that know it, some think us worthy to be cast into dungeons, yea, to be put to death for it, although they be not able, by the Scriptures of God, either to justify their own standing in their false ways, or to blame this our walking in the way of Christ. Others are fearful of the faces of men, or as forgetful of the afflictions of Joseph; not having, or at least not showing themselves to have the fellow feelings which ought to be in the members of the body, whereof Christ is the Head. And this our misery continueth, yet none at all put out their hands to help us, so that we may justly lament and say, as is written: 'They have shut up our life in the dungeon, and cast a stone upon us. Yea, for thy sake, O Lord, are we killed all day long, and are counted as sheep to the slaughter.' But, however

God for a time chastise our sins and try our faith, in stamping us under feet and in subverting our cause, and overthrowing our right before the face of Him that is high, yet certainly there is a time when this our warfare shall be accomplished.

"Remember, I beseech you (Right Honorable), that your Lord hath, by express commandment, laid this duty upon all His servants, to open their mouth in the cause of His children, especially when they are appointed unto destruction; and that He hath promised also, and will give, a plentiful blessing and reward to the performance hereof; and that your Lordship hath been many ways helpful to the distressed ministers of God, being yourself (through the mercy of God) an ancient professor and furtherer of the sincerity of the gospel for which we suffer. . . .

"On my knees I beseech your Lordship, by yourself, or the Earl of Essex, the Lord Grey, or such others, to be a means that this our petition may be delivered to Her Highness' hands; that we, finding favor in Her Majesty's eyes, through the blessing of God, this heavy drain laid upon our loins may be removed, and that we be not still forced to go into fire and water (as hitherto we have been), and that only for our obedience to the commandments of Christ; but that we may be suffered, together with peace, either to live under Her Majesty's government, in obedience of the gospel, in any place of her dominions (which we most desire), or else to depart whithersoever it shall please God to bring us, and to give us a resting-place for the service of His name, and in peace and tranquillity. . . .

"I am bold to send to your Lordship a short 'confession of faith' and an 'apology,' drawn by that faithful witness of Christ, our brother Penry, before his death. Although condemned of men, yet I doubt not but he was accepted of God, and now is partaker of that crown of life which is promised to all them that are faithful unto death. The poor remnant of Christians (who are falsely called Brownists) do all of us generally agree with our faithful brethren, in that confession of faith and allegiance to God and Her Majesty, as we have often adduced to the world. . . .

"Let it not be tedious to your Lordship, I beseech you, to read over this 'confession of faith,' which also may be shown to whom it pleaseth you. Only let me humbly entreat your Lordship not to make known from whom you received it; neither to show this, or any former letters, till it please God I be free out of prison, either alive or dead in the Lord.

"I scarce know any person, to whom your Lordship can show them, that will not make relation of it to the Prelate of Canterbury and other of our adversaries; who will the more, either continue my restraint in prison, or hasten the end of my days in this life. But I know your Lordship will be very careful hereof in these dangerous days. If it please God so to dispose, as there shall be nothing obtained from our former general suit to her Majesty, yet I humbly beseech your Lordship to be a means, either by yourself or the Earl of Essex, to Her Majesty's council or commissioners, to procure mine own liberty (there being now a new statute), if not, then under bail for four or five months this summer for the benefit of my health."*

In one of his "former letters," dated "from the *Clink*, January 8, 1593, and subscribed by himself as "pastor of that poor distressed church, and still in close prison for the gospel of Jesus Christ," Francis Johnson says to Lord Burghley: "If the session had been holden at Newgate at the beginning of last month, as was appointed, two of us (who are falsely called Brownists) were to be indicted.

"We are not within the danger of the statute of the 35 Eliz. cap. 1, whereupon we have thought they would indict us, much less of the statute of 23 Eliz. cap. 2."

Who they be that are indicted we cannot learn Mr. Wroth, one of the commissioners, openly spoke of it at Westminster, the fifth of last month, at

* Harleian MSS. 6849. 143.

which time also a preacher, Mr. Smyth, one of us, being called thither (eleven months a prisoner, and yet in the Marshalsea).

"I know (Right Honorable)," he continues, "we are a people despised and reviled of all men. Yea, everywhere spoken against as schismatics, seditious persons, subverters of the state, and what not. But this (alas!) hath been the lot of the truth and servants of God everywhere. Yea, of the prophets, apostles, and of Christ himself, thus to be railed upon and persecuted for the truth's sake; and commonly, under other color and pretence. Therefore, we are not ashamed of the gospel and sufferings of Christ. We suffer for laboring, in all holy and peaceable manner, to obey our Lord Jesus Christ in His own ordinances, ministry, and worship, prescribed in His last testament, and sealed with His precious blood.

"If we err in these things, prisons and the gallows are no fit means to convince and persuade our consciences, but rather a quiet and godly conference, or a discussion of the matter by writing, before equal and impartial judges. This we have often sued for, but could never obtain. We now, therefore, in a humble manner, solicit your Lordship to procure this for us. We are fully persuaded of this from the word of God, and are ready, by the grace of God, to seal it with our own blood. But we desire it, that the truth being discovered and made manifest, the false offices, callings, livings, and possessions of the prelacy, might be converted to Her Majesty's use, as were, not long since, the livings of the abbots, monks, and friars in these dominions; and that by these means the gospel of Christ may have free course, and the peace of the church be promoted."

The father of Francis Johnson, who was mayor of Richmond, in Yorkshire, exerted himself to secure the freedom of his two sons (both confined in the Clink).

"When our poor old father applied to Justice Young," Francis says, "for us to have the liberty of the prison, he and the Dean of Westminster would have sent him to prison, had not Justice Barnes interposed and prevented them."

An original manuscript in the handwriting of the "poor old father" is still in existence. The subjoined is a copy:

"The humble petition of John Johnson for his two sons, Francis and George Johnson, having been close prisoners; the one in the Clink a year and a half, and the other in the Fleet sixteen months, only for their conscience in religion.

"To the Right Honorable the Lord High Treasurer of England:

"Most humbly sueth to your Lordship, your poor suitor, John Johnson, to have in remembrance the petition he referred to your honor in behalf of his two sons, Francis and George Johnson, who have been kept close prisoners, the one in the Clink a year and a half, the other in the Fleet sixteen months, only for that upon conscience they refuse to have spiritual communion with the present ministry of the land. Both of these have been scholars and masters of arts in the University of Cambridge, and there brought up in learning to the great charges of your orator, their father, who with all the suit he can make to Her Majesty's high commissioners, finding no release for his sons, is enforced to make his humble suit unto your honor; beseeching your honorable and Christian help (your said orator being shortly to return unto the north country where he dwelleth), that his sons may either be discharged altogether, or have the benefit which the preachers had two years since, who, being prisoners, were suffered to be at some honest men's houses in the city, upon sufficient assurance there to be forthcoming upon warning duly given,* and that (till this be effected) they may for their health and lessening of their

* Cartwright in a letter to Lord Grey, says his fellow-prisoners in the Clink and White Lyon, had obtained from His Grace of Canterbury this liberty, by their own bond of forty pounds, on the condition of returning to their prisons at night. See Landsdowne MSS. 69, art. 40.

charges, have the liberty of the prisons where they are; and the younger, called George, be removed from the Fleet, where he hath been most unchristianly entreated, so as he hath been kept, sometimes two days and two nights together, without any manner of sustenance. Sometimes twenty nights together without any bedding, save a straw mat, and as long without any change of linen. And all this sixteen months in the most dark and unwholesome rooms of the prison they could thrust him into, not suffering any of his friends to come unto him; and now of late, not permitting your orator, his father, so much as to see him.

"In all which respects your poor suppliant is forced, even in the bowels of nature and of the Lord Jesus Christ, to sue to your honor, that it would please you, by your honor's good means to see that release may be had of the most unhealthful, chargeable, and long-continued close imprisonment of his two sons aforesaid; and thus, both he and they shall be bound daily to pray unto God for Her Majesty and your honor's health and happiness in this life and for ever. 1 July, 1594."

These overtures on behalf of Francis Johnson and his brother were not attended with immediate success. Francis was left in bonds; but, amidst the privations and dreariness of the Clink prison, he found opportunity to write in exposition and in the defence of his principles.

"There was a gentlewoman,"* we are told, "imprisoned because she would not join with the public ministry, in England, in the worship of God." To justify her course, and withstand the importunity of her friends, she gave a reason for her faith in a letter to Arthur Hildersham, a Puritan minister of great report. The reply of Hildersham she sent to Francis Johnson, in prison, to be answered by him with more ability than she possessed.

The tedium of imprisonment was also relieved by a discussion which originated, apparently, with Mr. Daniel Buck, one of the members of the church who was taken prisoner in the woods at Islington.

This capture and imprisonment, together with the martyrdom of the faithful ministers, greatly staggered Mr. Buck. He was a kind of small banker in the borough of Southwark, and had begun to taste the sweets of prosperity.

The thought, either of capital punishment or of

---

* There is some probability that this "gentlewoman" entered into nearer relation with the pastor in bonds who undertook the defence of her principles. However this may be, Francis Johnson was married to a lady of whom the Pilgrim Fathers speak in terms of respect and admiration. She had a "good estate, and was a godly woman, very modest both in her apparel and all her demeanor, ready to any good works in her place, and helpful to many, especially the poor, and an ornament to his calling."

perpetual exile, was extremely unwelcome to his mind; for he was one of a numerous class, by no means extinct, who doubt the utility of martyrdom under any circumstances. Combining with the instinct of self-preservation the sagacity of a man of business, Mr. Buck hit upon the expedient of trying to persuade his minister, Francis Johnson, to accommodate his conscience to the act of parliament, so that the troubles of imprisonment might, for the future, be avoided, and all the brethren be left in peace and comfort to pursue their worldly callings.

He knew too well the sternness of principle in his pastor to try, in a direct manner, to reduce him to a compromise; but it occurred to him that, with the aid of Mr. Henry Jacob, a clergyman at Cheriton, in the neighboring county of Kent, the change he desired might be effected. He proposed, in a disputation between them, to act as messenger; taking the papers to Johnson in prison from Jacob, and returning to and fro with propositions, replies, and rejoinders, according to the particular turn of the controversy. Mr. Buck was quite satisfied with the reasoning of Henry Jacob, though evidently disappointed in the issue. He published the paper "to show the obstinate dealing of Master Johnson."

The discussion was protracted and of varied character. The *argumentum ad hominem* was more freely used than would be deemed courteous in modern times.

"I pray you, Master Johnson," writes Henry Jacob, "consider yourself. You were a true Christian before you fell into this separation. Moreover, you were learned. You knew and acknowledged those very corruptions a great while, and yet condemned us not. Nay, you condemned this separation earnestly. I pray you, is it not possible that numbers, who see not so far as you did then, should still condemn your separation, and yet be true Christians, as you acknowledge that yourself then was; *me ipso teste?*

"That which you add of persecution unto bonds and exile and death, to prove our utter abolishing from Christ generally, it is a toy. First, if you were merely innocent, yet this could not make us worse than the Jews in Christ's time; yet for all that they persecuted were not wholly fallen from God. Secondly, you suffer, indeed, more than you need, if that you would but acknowledge the grace of God with us, so far as it is. It is, therefore, not Christ's cross, in that regard, but your own, that you bear."

"I confess," replies Johnson, " that whiles I was minister and member of your church, in that constitution I stood in an antichristian state, yet doubt I not but even then, being of the elect of God, I was partaker, through faith, of the mercy of God in Christ, to salvation; and this, I hope, is the case of divers among you. But, for myself, I have now the more assurance, in that God hath both drawn me out of that antichristian state, giving me more to see and forsake it, and hath planted me in His true church and household, giving me to receive His truth in much affection, with joy of the Holy Ghost. But, as for you in your estate, besides that you are not members of any true visible church, you do, moreover, abide in gross confusion, false ministry, antichristian worship, and other abominations, by the word of God already discovered. Now, whiles you thus remain, you cannot, in that estate, approve yourself to have the promise of salvation, whereof, by the word of God, you can be assured, until you depart out of that Babylon, and save yourself from that froward generation.

"You so carry yourself as if you had been chaplain to Bonner, Bancroft, Gardiner, Whitgift, or some such Caiaphas; and so testify that not only the Prelates and Formalists, but even the Reformists, among whom you reckon yourself, have your hands in our blood, consenting and approving that which is done against us.

"You say we suffer more than we need. Did not Bonner often so speak of the martyrs? What think you also of the sufferings of Mr. Udale, Mr. Fenner,

Mr. Dearing, and Mr. Merbury ? Show us in what particulars we suffer more than we need. We suffer only for bearing witness to the truth of Christ against the abominations of antichrist."

Henry Jacob asked his opponent what difference he put between the Church of England and the martyrs of the Marian persecution.

In reply, Johnson said :

" 1. Greater light of the truth is now come into the world than was in those days, but you love darkness more than light, for you still walk in darkness.

" 2. They witnessed against the abominations of antichrist (then called in question) to the loss of their liberty and lives. Your church doth not so against the remnants of popery (now controverted), but do either openly defend them, or fearfully submit to them.

" 3. They consisted not of all sorts of people, good and bad, as your church doth.

" 4. Such of them as were ministers were degraded from their antichristian functions. So do not yours.

They were (members), and died members of a true and visible church (namely, that persecuted church, in Queen Mary's day, which was separated from the rest of the land, as from the world, and formed together in the fellowship of the gospel by voluntary submission thereunto; though, in that time of ignorance, they had their defects and errors). You continue members of a falsely constituted church, unseparated from the world, yielding subjection to antichristian enormities against the ordinances of Jesus Christ."

Henry Jacob reminded his antagonist that, amongst those who separated from the church, there were many who held erroneous opinions, and that in his own church there was not perfect agreement.

Francis Johnson admitted that there was weakness and imperfection in the members. They were, he said, but newly come out of Babylon. There was contention and error in the primitive church, until they were duly sifted. "There may be sundry things," he added, "wherein the brethren of the same church may differ in judgment among themselves, and yet, notwithstanding, walk together in the same faith, testimony, and fellowship, wherein God hath united their minds, none of them being contentious to disquiet the church or the members thereof, and all being ready to receive the truth which God by His word shall further make known whatsoever it be;* and thus, I dare boldly say that, whosoever

---

* The student of Pilgrim History will be reminded of the terms of the church covenant quoted by Robinson, twenty-five years after, in his parting advice on the sailing of the Speedwell from Holland: "We promise and covenant with God and one with an other, to receive whatsoever light or truth shall be made known to us from his written word."

shall not thus hold and walk, they shall not only condemn the apostles and primitive churches, together with the martyrs, but shall find by experience, that neither any churches, nor so much as two or three men shall ever be able to keep fellowship any while together among themselves."

We have no need to follow the discussion further. Francis Johnson remained true to his convictions, and was, as we have seen, exposed for his "obstinacy."

Henry Jacob did not forget the powerful strokes of his opponent. He was not satisfied with his own position, but he looked for a scriptural reformation in the church of England in the course of Providence, and hesitated, as others like-minded did, in view of the cross to be taken up in unreserved obedience to the truth. Henry Ainsworth and John Smyth, of whom we shall hear further, halted between two opinions. Ainsworth went to Ireland, and was occupied in missionary labors. Smyth, on his liberation from the Marshalsea, because of failing health, spent some time in conference with friends. Francis Johnson went forward in the narrow, rugged, and difficult path. We have no distinct information respecting the judicial proceedings in his case, but we learn, incidentally, that in the first instance he was banished to Newfoundland.

More than two centuries and a half have passed

away since then, adding little to the attractions of that distant shore as a place of exile. What must have been the isolation of one transported there before the close of the sixteenth century? Yet Johnson was not alone in that penal settlement for "the people falsely called Brownists." Four of his brethren and companions, as they shared the same fate, were brought into closer fellowship, and were cheered and strengthened by mutual sympathies.

All who had pined for years in the dungeons were not suffered to go into exile. Saxio Bellot and Robert Bowle, indicted with Barrowe and Greenwood, were respited, as offenders of a "more pardonable degree." But their escape from the gallows was only to be subjected to a more lingering death in prison. With many others they sank from want and the fetid atmosphere.

Christopher Bowman, one of their number, in a petition still in existence, describes their terrible sufferings. In some cases the record is, that the prisoner "being sick unto death was carried forth and ended his life within a day or two after." Aged Christian women were amongst the victims. In the "dark and cloudy day" it is almost impossible to trace the course of the flock of slaughter.

The members were scattered in various parts of the country; and the brethren in "Norwich, Gloucester, and Bury," endured like afflictions with the church in London.

X.

THE SECOND SEPARATION. — BREWSTER AND THE CHURCH AT SCROOBY MANOR.

HOLLAND, the land of windmills, dykes, and treckskuyts, is not famed for natural scenery.

The distinction of the poet, —

"Man made the town, God made the country,"

scarcely applies where the banks and hillocks are so artificial. Pictorial objects are not wanting, as the Dutch painters have proved, but they are found chiefly in browsing cattle, or in peasantry in a state of easy indulgence, dozing in the shade, or yielding to the influence of quiet conviviality. Yet the traveller may visit, by the light of the harvest-moon, a part of Amsterdam with feelings of interest almost entrancing. The antique houses with high gables, the stately trees reflected in the waters of the street canals, the lights in the boats of the fishermen, and the silvery rays of the moon thrown over the river, produce an effect which will linger in the memory as pleasantly as that of some beautiful lake imbosomed in the mountains, or as the windings of the Rhine. In this "city of refuge" the English exiles, for conscience' sake, found a resting place at the close of the sixteenth century. The exact time of their arrival is unknown to us, nor can we tell the order in which they came.

This only is certain: that in a "blind lane" of Amsterdam a church was formed under the pastoral care of Francis Johnson and Henry Ainsworth, who were associated with Daniel Studley, Stanshall Mercer, George Kugorton, Thomas Bishop, and David Bresto, as elders or representatives. Their names will be familiar to the reader in connection with the trials and persecutions endured by them in London. Ainsworth says: "We being called of God, whiles we dwelt in England, entered into covenant there, and became His church and people, and so had equal right in Christ, His gospel and ordinances, with all churches in the world."

The quiet of the exiled church was only comparative. Influential parties in England tried to excite suspicion in the minds of their neighbors, and they were represented as holding dangerous principles, and as disorderly in practice. Unhappily, whilst exposed to vigilant and unfriendly scrutiny from without, they were tried, in no small degree, by the weakness and restlessness of some of their own company.

" For this cause," they say, " hath our exile been

hardly thought of by many, and evil spoken of by some. . . . Without all further search they have accounted and divulged us as heretics or schismatics, at the least; yea some, and such as worst might, have sought the increase of our afflictions even here also, if they could; which they have both secretly and openly attempted." For the information, therefore, of all churches, they gave a distinct "confession of faith," confirming every position by citations from Scripture. They made, also, their appeal to posterity. " However," they say, " this present generation shall judge of these things, yet the age to come (which will be less partial) will easily give sentence. . . . The crime of heresy is not to be imputed to them whose faith doth wholly rely upon most sure ground of Scripture. They are not schismatics who entirely cleave to the true church of God, such as the prophets and apostles describe unto us; nor are they to be counted sectaries who embrace the truth of God which is one and always like itself."

They entered into a polemical correspondence with the learned Francis Junius, but with little effect, so far as he was personally concerned. He stood upon his dignity, and was careful to retain the respect of the Anglican prelates. " If ye have found a place of rest," writes the Dutch professor, " ye shall do wisely, if ye do not stir where ye may be in quiet. . . . Pity yourselves, your flock, your entertainers, the whole church." The pacific Junius was evidently of opinion that they should have been content to breathe without daring to think. The exiled confessors had not, however, been tamed down to this point of passive quiescence. The appeal made to their regard for self-preservation found no response from men who had "suffered the loss of all things."

"If you write again," said the exiles to Junius, "we do humbly and earnestly entreat, if anywhere we have erred in our faith and cause, that you vouchsafe to show it us by the word of God. . . . Pity, we pray you, our church here exiled, everywhere reproached, eaten up, in a manner, with deep poverty, despised and afflicted well near of all; against which Satan hath now, for a long time, attempted all utmost extremities. Pity them from whom we have departed, who, under pretence of the gospel, continue still in antichristian defection."

The writings of Ainsworth and Johnson attracted great attention, and, in spite of the efforts made by the bishops to prevent their circulation, they were read, in different parts of England, with great avidity; and, we may presume, no doubt exerted an influence in determining the course of some who had hesitated in doubt and misgiving.

At the close of the reign of Elizabeth, the Separatists, who remained in their native land, were left, for a time, unmolested. John Smyth, the pupil of Francis Johnson at Cambridge, and subsequently, as we have seen, a prisoner in the Marshalsea, now exercised his ministry at Gainsboro' in Lincolnshire. In 1602, he formed a Christian society, the members of which, "as the Lord's free people, joined themselves (by a covenant of the Lord) unto a church estate, in the fellowship of the gospel, to walk in all His ways made known, or to be made known unto them, according to their best endeavors, whatever it should cost them."

John Robinson, M. A., of Corpus Christi College, Cambridge, gave in his adhesion to their cause, and they became known as the "Brethren of the Second Separation."

Joseph Hale (afterwards Bishop) attributes the change in the sentiments of Robinson to the influence of Smyth. "Lincolnshire," he says, "was your country, and Master Smyth your oracle and general." But in the account of his conversion to these views, given by himself, he refers to the writings of Barrowe, Greenwood, and Penry, as instrumental in the change. The style of these earnest men, we might have supposed, would be repellent, in some degree, to the more sober taste of Robinson; but he justly observes: "Whatsoever truth is in the world, it is from God, and from Him we have it, by what hand soever it be reached unto us. 'Came the word of God unto you only?'" 1 Cor. xiv. 36.

Robinson admits that he had been restrained from the avowal of his convictions by too great deference to the Puritan divines. "I do willingly acknowledge their learning and godliness," he says, "and do honor the memory of some of them; yet I neither think them so learned but they might err, nor so godly, but in their error they might reproach the truth they saw not. I do, indeed, confess, to the glory of God and mine own shame, that a long time before I entered this way, I took some taste of the truth in some treatises published in justification of it, which, the Lord knoweth, were as sweet as honey unto my mouth; and the very principal thing which, for the time, quenched all further appetite in me, was the overvaluation which I made of the learning and holiness of these and the like persons; blushing in myself to have a thought of pressing one hairbreadth before them in this thing, behind whom I knew myself to come so many miles in all other things. Yea, and even of later times, when I had entered into a more serious consideration of these things, and according to the measure of grace received, searched the Scriptures whether they were so or no, and, by searching, found much light of truth; yet was the same so dimmed and overclouded with the contradictions of these men and others of like note, that had not the truth been in my heart as a burning fire, shut up in my bones (Jer. xx. 9), I had never broken those bonds of flesh and blood wherein I was so straitly tied, but had suffered the light of God to have been put out in mine own unthankful heart by other men's darkness.'

We can never know the secret mental struggles of the men who, like Robinson, left their former associations, in obedience to the truth, and connected themselves with a few poor and despised people who sought to advance principles dearer to them than life itself. The contemptuous and scurrilous terms in which even Hale, the author of the "Contemplations," could indulge in speaking of them, may give us some idea of the scorn and contumely they had to bear.

Richard Clifton, rector of Babworth, relinquished his living to identify himself with the cause of the Separatists. The change in his sentiments was also attributed to the influence of John Smyth.

Though disturbed by these secessions from the establishment, the opponents of the Separatists ridiculed them for the paucity of their numbers.

"Some one prison," said Hale, "might hold all your refined flock." "We look not," they replied, "in any case, to the greatest number either of people or elders, but in all cases we look to God's law and testimony, as we are commanded, which, when it is showed, by whomsoever, all ought to yield unto. We know neither the multitude, neither yet the mighty or rabbis are still to be followed. There are differences of gifts and offices in the church. Yet no man's gift or office (no, not though he were an angel from heaven) may carry us from the written word, by which the godly people tried even the apostle's doctrine, and were commended."

More of the Puritan ministers would have joined the brethren of the second separation, but for the severity of the penalty incurred by the step. Richard Bernard, vicar of Worksop, at one time inclined this way. "I doubt not but Mr. Bernard," said Robinson, "and a thousand more ministers in the land, were they secure of the magistrate's sword, and might they go on with his good license, would wholly shake off their canonical obedience to their ordinaries, and neglect their citations and censures, and refuse to sue in their courts, for all the peace of the church which they commend to us for so sacred a thing, could they but obtain license from the magistrates to use their liberty which they are persuaded Christ had given them,— they would soon shake off the prelates' yoke, and draw no longer under the same in spiritual communion with all the profane in the land, but would break their bonds of iniquity as easily as Samson did the cord wherewith Delilah tied him, and give good reasons also from the word of God for their so doing. And yet the approbation of men and angels makes the ways of God and works of religion never a whit the more lawful, but only the more free from bodily labor."

Such teaching made its impression in the district. Bernard, to accommodate matters, formed an inner circle of Christian people in his parish, who adopted a "covenant." But for such practices he lost his vicarage. And it became needful, in order to regain episcopal favor, that he should prove himself a more thorough-going churchman. He wrote bitterly against Smyth. The discussion between them is curious, and not without interest, but to follow its windings would be almost to lose the thread of our narrative.

The church at Gainsboro' increased in number and became two bands. A second, or branch church, was formed at Scrooby, about twelve miles distant.

The brethren were received to the house of William Brewster, formerly in the service of Secretary Davison, and now postmaster, occupying the manor house at Scrooby. His old mansion (once the temporary residence of Cardinal Wolsey, and coveted by King James as a hunting box, when he "took his pleasure" in Sherwood forest) afforded good accommodation for the church. Here they met and enjoyed the pastoral care, first of Richard Clifton, and then that of John Robinson. Brewster showed them great kindness. He was a man of large and varied experience, and well acquainted with persons of eminent piety and Christian usefulness in different parts of the country. It is probable that he was indebted for his appointment as postmaster to the influence of Lady Stanhope, a woman of most exemplary character. William Bradford, an orphan youth, living with his uncle in the neighboring hamlet of Austerfield, joined the church soon after its formation. His mind had been deeply impressed under the ministry of Richard Clifton, and he resolved, in his seventeenth year, to cast in his lot with the people who met in Scrooby manor. He wished, he said, "to engage with some society of the faithful, that should keep close unto the written word of God, as the rule of their worship." His uncles were strongly opposed, but in answer to their remonstrances, he said: "To keep a good conscience, and walk in such a way as God has prescribed in His word, is a thing which I shall prefer above you all, and above life itself."

These village Christians were much encouraged by the letters of the pastor of the church at Gainsboro'. "Brethren," he writes, "you are few in number, yet, considering that the kingdom of heaven is as a grain of mustard seed, small in the beginning, yet I do not doubt but you may, in time, grow up to a multitude, and be, as it were, a great tree full of fruitful branches. The truth now, blessed be the Lord, is so evident, that all the men upon earth can never be able to quench it."

As he penned these semi-prophetic words, John Smyth had no idea that in the church of the manor house was the germ of a nation now consisting of thirty millions. Probably, at the outset, the hope was indulged that their Christian society would not be disturbed. The accession of James to the throne of England raised the hopes of the more advanced Puritans. Petitions were prepared indeed by the Separatists, under the illusion that the prince, who had made such pious professions, would recognize their right to worship God as they were persuaded by His word. Henry Jacob seems to have been one of the most sanguine as to the gracious intentions of the new monarch. He exerted himself to procure signatures to the Millenary petition. The evidence of his zeal, in promoting, is supplied in his manuscripts at Lambeth. But he proceeded a few steps further in the direction of the Separatists, and appealed to the King, as the "noblest pillar of the gospel," in favor of complete reformation. With innocent simplicity he says: "We have had it from your Majesty very oft, that whatsoever things in our churches we can show to be contrary to God's word, shall be by your gracious means removed, and whatsoever (yet out of use with us) may appeal by God's word to be necessary, shall be established. We crave, we desire nothing more."

It is curious and very interesting to observe that the arguments addressed to Henry Jacob, by Francis Johnson from the Clink prison, were now adopted by him in almost the same terms, in reasoning with the pedantic monarch; and he candidly admits that he had long been convinced by them. The King, however, was not so impressible.

On the 24th of October, 1603, he issued a proclamation, in which he "commanded all his subjects not to publish any thing against the state ecclesiastical, or to gather subscriptions or make supplications, being resolved to make it appear by their chastisement how far such a manner of proceedings was disagreeable to him; for he was determined to preserve the ecclesiastical state in such form as he found it established by law, only to reform such abuses as should be apparently proved."

Under pretence of arguing the case, the famous conference was held at the palace of Hampton Court, January 14, 16, and 18, 1604. The Puritan ministers, insulted and browbeaten, were denuded of all hope of concession. "I will have," said the King, "one doctrine, one discipline, one religion in substance and ceremony. Never speak more to that point, how far you are bound to obey." After the speech of Dr. Reynolds, on the second day, the King replied:

"If this be all your party have to say, I will make them conform, or I will harry them out of this land, or else worse."

On the third day the temper of the gloomy monarch was not in the slightest degree improved. "I will have none of this arguing," he said, sternly, "therefore let them conform, and that quickly too, or they shall hear of it; the bishops will give them some time, but if any are of an obstinate and turbulent spirit, I will have them enforced to conformity."

The bishops allowed little breathing time to those who would not conform. Henry Jacob, known to be a prime mover of the Millenary petition, was naturally selected as one of the first to be tamed into submission. The mode of procedure on the part of the bishop was characteristic. He sent for Henry Jacob to the palace, as if for a friendly interview, and then, having sent his guest to ruminate in the Clink prison, he gave direction to the pursuivant to go to his dwelling-house in Woodside, Cheapside, and seize his papers. By the light of some of these original documents we learn particulars that would otherwise be lost. In a letter to the Bishop of London, Henry Jacob says that, in giving expression to his views, he had only accepted the invitation of the King. "We are condemned by many," he adds, "and verily we ought to be, as schismatics and contentious persons, if we will differ from you, and yet give forth unto the world no reasons for the difference. While we were silent and did nothing, we were insulted for a long time together. Now, when one of us doth give some reasons with due respect, it is an offence to do it." He closes the letter in these terms: " I came to your Lordship freely, without commandment, when my servant told me your messenger, that your Lordship would speak with me, so I beseech you deal kindly with me. I beseech you restore me to my poor wife and four small children, who, without my enlargement, are in much distress. Your Lordship's humble suppliant, Henry Jacob, prisoner in the Clink."

The struggle between conscience and natural affection was severe. Many times Henry Jacob tried to frame terms of submission, which should be consistent with his sense of duty, and yet secure his freedom. These documents in the rough draft are still preserved. He gave bail to remain silent for a time. This was dangerous ground. To escape from the temptation to impound the truth and to prevaricate, he went to Holland, and soon found there John Smyth and Richard Clifton, with the brethren from London, who had retired to that country some years before.

XI.

PERSECUTIONS. MRS. CHURCHMAN.

We return to Scrooby. Even to-day it retains its primitive listlessness and insignificance. A more perfect picture of still life could hardly be found. Austerfield is equally languid. The two villages are connected with the river Idle, a glassy stream, an appropriate emblem in character and in name of the quiet district. That men of such firmness, energy, and decision as the Pilgrim fathers, should have sprung from a locality like this, only shows the power of Christian truth to give stamina and force to character, when all external influences have a tendency entirely opposite. Yet it is very possible, that the members of the little church would have all sunk into the oblivion, common to their neighbors in all preceding generations, if persecution had not driven them into fame. How persons so moderate and socially harmless could have provoked such hostility, as that evinced by their possessors, is marvellous.

We are told, in a general way, that "they were hunted

and persecuted on every side, so as their former afflictions were but as mole-hills to mountains, in comparison to these which now came upon them. Some were taken and clapped up in prisons, others had their houses beset and watched night and day, and hardly escaped their heads; and the most were fain to fly and leave their houses and habitations and the means of their livelihood."

Interesting, however, as are all the statements of Bradford, it is sometimes rather mortifying that he does not enter into a little further detail. We feel as if we should like to question some of the " ancient men," on points relative to their religious life at Scrooby and its vicinity. The recital of Christian experience given by persecuted nonconformists, at a later period, may suggest to us some idea of the troubles and vicissitudes to which the Pilgrims were subjected.

We have before us a simple and touching record of the trials of Mrs. Mary Churchman, in the seventeenth century, which in its main features, no doubt, would correspond with the story of one of the Pilgrim mothers, if we could hear it as from her own lips. Originally, she tells us, she was "zealous for the established church," and that she had " as great an inclination to persecute as Paul had." The means she resorted to for the annoyance of schismatics were not quite so terrible, however, as those employed by

Saul of Tarsus. "There lay a way," she tells us, "through my father's yard, for Mrs. M., a godly woman, to go to meeting, which she did every Lord's day. I really thought it my duty to set his great dog to molest her, and used sometimes to encourage him, for half a mile together, with the most bitter invectives. Yet such was the preventing providence of God, that he never fastened upon this gracious person.

"When about eighteen years of age, it pleased the Lord to lay on me a languishing fit of sickness, which raised in me some promises of a new life."

On her recovery, she was persuaded by a pious neighbor to go with her to meeting. His preaching, she says, "made me tremble and secretly wish I have never come there. This trouble I vented in floods of tears, for now thought I, they will think me one of themselves, which I at that time was fully resolved against. I seemed now to like their persons worse than ever. In great hurry and confusion I sat till service was ended. After sermon, staying for my neighbor, the minister came to me, and asked where I lived? who I was? and whether I knew any thing of the Lord Jesus Christ?"

She returned blind answers, and was very angry with her friend for bringing her to such a place.

The desire, nevertheless, arose in her mind to attend the service again. With joy and thankfulness she discovered in the Lord Jesus a hiding place, and could scarcely refrain from expressing aloud the delight she experienced.

It was, therefore, by the attractive and subduing influence of the truth, that hearers were drawn to these "conventicles." All who came had to "count the cost." But we must hear the sequel: "My father was then high constable, and had an order from the justices to return all the names of them who frequented the meetings. This made it a hard thing for his own daughter to be a fanatic, which was what he could not bear; and this also increased my difficulty in getting out on the Lord's day, which, notwithstanding, I sometimes did, and have walked eight, ten, yea twelve miles to meeting. If my father at any time understood where I was gone, he spent the day in nothing but oaths and curses and resolves to murder me. My mother, though an enemy to fanatics, would frequently send a servant to meet me before I could reach home, to tell me not to appear till my father was gone to bed; and I often hid myself in a wood-stack, where I have seen him pass by, with a naked knife in his hand, declaring he would kill me before he slept." After an account of various changes and trials, Mrs. Churchman says: "Persecution now came on apace; the dissenters could have no meetings but in woods and corners. I myself have seen our companies often alarmed with drums and soldiers; every one was fined five pounds a month for being in their company. Here God left me to stagger; Satan suggested if you give your body to be burned, and have not *charity*, it is nothing, 2 Cor. xiii. 3. But the greater the temptation, the greater was the deliverance from those words, Rev. vii. 14: 'These are they which came out of great tribulation, and have washed their robes, and made them white in the blood of the Lamb.'

"Mr. B., with whom I lived, had a call to Holland, and as the persecution was very threatening in England, he thought it his duty to accept the call. He gave me an invitation to go with him, assuring me that all things should be in common.

"As I well knew my circumstances were very precarious, not having anywhere to hide my head, when this worthy family was gone, this drew me into great straits. I sought the Lord time after time on this account, and it seemed as if He was providing for me in another land. Grace taught me my duty to my parents, though they were enemies to the cross of Christ. Accordingly I acquainted them with this invitation, and that I should comply with it, unless their commands were to the contrary. I added, in my letter, I should be all obedient to them, saving in matters relating to my God, and though I had not been permitted to see them seven years past, yet could assure them, my affections for them were the same as ever. I begged they would consider of it, and let me know in eight days' time, for all things were ready to embark in a fortnight.

"Not hearing from them in the time I set, I took their silence for a consent, and so prepared all things ready for my journey, and set out with my kind friends. Just before we reached Harwich, where we were to take shipping, a messenger from my father overtook me with a letter, the contents of which were as follows: That if I would come home, I should have my liberty to worship God in my own way, but as to my leaving the land, this was what they could not bear, therefore without fail I must come back with the messenger; which I did. Great was the sorrow of parting with my friends, but my duty to my parents surmounted all.

"I no sooner entered my father's house but my mother, in receiving me, fainted away. My father also, though a man of great spirit, offered to fall on his knees, to ask my pardon for his former cruelty. Oh, amazing work of sovereign grace! My father immediately told me, I should have my liberty in matters relating to my God. I then humbly offered my obedience to them both on my knees. At supper there was not a mouthful eaten but with tears. I well knew my God had appeared to my father on my behalf, as he did to Laban of old, and applied Jacob's promise to myself, Gen. xxxii. 12: 'Thou saidst I will surely do thee good.' The next Sabbath, my father came into my chamber by break of day, and told me I should have a horse and a man to wait on me to the meeting." The writer of the narrative relates the conversion of the whole family, but we limit our extracts from it to the passages that illustrate the trials of Christian people in a condition similar to those of the church at Scrooby. Walking over the gently undulating fields between Scrooby and Austerfield, we may imagine how these companions in the faith and patience of Jesus, young and old, would have to tell of hair-breadth escapes from constables, the seizure of friends, their wanderings in quest of employment, the privations suffered from the loss of means by fines, and the keener sorrows arising from the opposition and displeasure of their kindred who were averse to the course they felt it an imperative duty to pursue.

And yet they had a present recompense. The truth became to them a heart necessity. They prized Christian ordinances above life itself, and they derived from them consolation and support of which the world knows nothing. Their constancy, no doubt, often led to inquiry on the part of relatives and neighbors who were before estranged. In some instances their oppressors, subdued by their meekness and gentleness, confessed their error and sought to be instructed in principles, the effect of which, on their character and spirit, they witnessed with glowing admiration. "We will go with you," they had to say, "for we have heard that God is with you."

Hallowed and delightful were their meetings for worship and conference at the Manor-house. With "great love" elder Brewster "entertained them when they came, making provision for them to his great charge."

XII.

DIFFICULTIES IN REACHING HOLLAND.

THE moors of England are peculiar to the country. They differ from the uncleared lands of America and from uncultivated regions in other parts of the world. In the summer season, or in the bright days of autumn, a ramble over them is pleasant and invigorating.

The fine bracing air, scented with the bloom of wild flowers, gives buoyancy to the pedestrian, and he enjoys a freedom from restraint he can find neither in the city nor village. The scene is changed in the winter, and woe to the stranger who is benighted or overtaken with the snow-storm.

The sheep tracks are filled up, the distant lights only add to his perplexity. He is in danger of stumbling over rocks or of sinking into a pool of standing water, and if he can once reach human dwellings he may be thankful, though it should be within some miles of his intended destination.

Between Grimsby and Hull there was an extensive moor in the days of the Pilgrims, skirted by the sea-shore, "a good way distant from any town." One evening, in the spring of 1608, there might have been seen a small boat full of women and children in a creek at the edge of this large common.

The appearance of such a party in a place so solitary and unfrequented was, in itself, no ordinary occurrence. The incident is explained by the fact that this company consisted of the wives, sisters, and children of the Pilgrims who had resolved to make their way to Holland. This was not their first attempt to escape. A year before, an engagement was made with a captain to convey them from Boston to the coast of Holland. On that occasion they embarked with all their goods under cover of night, but they were cruelly deceived. Instead of meeting them at the appointed time, the perfidious captain, though he had received the money of the Pilgrims, apprised the authorities of their intention to escape, and entered into a plot to capture them, with the aid of officers, when they should come on board in the evening. The disappointment, loss, and anxiety occasioned by this betrayal may be imagined. The books of Elder Brewster were seized with other effects. The Pilgrim passengers were turned out of the vessel into open boats, and, after a procession through the town, amidst the jeers of the mob, they were taken before the magistrates, who put them in ward for a month, and then committed seven of their leaders to prison for trial at the assizes.*

After this bitter experience, the best efforts of the Pilgrims were directed to secure embarkation at a place in which they should escape observation, and be free from interruption. They sailed in a small bark to the point fixed for receiving the passengers. The plan failed, for the Dutch captain did not come at the time expected. The rocking of the sea affected the women and children in the boat. For relief they sailed up the creek to smoother waters. Next day the captain made his appearance, but as the tide was out the bark could not go off to

* In connection with these magisterial proceedings, Toby Matthew, Archbishop of York, in the return made to the Exchequer on the 13th of November, 1608, of the fines which had been imposed within his diocese in the preceding year, for the purpose of the fines being levied, inserted the following: "Richard Jackson, William Brewster, and Robert Rochester, of Scrooby, in the county of Nottingham, Brownists or Separatists, for a fine or amercement of 20*l.* apiece, set and imposed upon every one of them by Robert Abbot and Robert Snowden, Doctors of Divinity, and Matthew Dodsworth, Bachelor of Law, commissioners for causes ecclesiastical within the province of York, for not appearing before them upon lawful summons at the Collegiate church of Southwell, the 22d day of April, Anno Domini, 1608,— 60*l.*

The two clerical commissioners were advanced to the episcopate. Abbot became Bishop of Salisbury. Snowden was afterwards Bishop of Carlisle. Mr. Hunter, the accomplished antiquary, to whom we are indebted for these particulars, is careful to tell us that the commissioners acted legally.

the ship. The skipper sent to fetch off the passengers, but scarcely had he received the first boat load on board, and was preparing to go for others, when he saw an armed rabble, horsemen and footmen, in the distance, rushing furiously to the rendezvous of the Pilgrims to capture them as at Boston.

Alarmed for his own safety, the captain, with an oath, ordered the men to weigh the anchor, set the sails, and put to sea. No time was given either for the men in the ship to receive the necessary supplies for the voyage, or for the women and children to join them.

The furious constables and "catchpoles" sprung upon their prey, and, regardless of the cries of the women and children, dragged them from the boat, and drove them across the common, destitute and shivering with cold, to make sport for their ignorant tormentors.

It was well after all, that the feebler portion of their company had been pent up in the creek, and so prevented from sailing, for the ship encountered terrific storms. For seven days, Bradford tells us, they "neither saw sun, moon, nor stars, and were driven to the coast of Norway. All on board seem to have given themselves up for lost, at one time, but after their fears and troubles, they reached the desired haven."

The watchful eye of Providence was over the

defenceless mothers and their children left behind. They were hurried from one justice to another until their oppressors were fairly wearied, and "were glad to be rid of them in the end upon any terms."

After "turmoiling a good while," says the faithful narrator, "necessity forced a way for them."

This fruit came from all their public troubles. "Their cause became famous, and occasioned many to look into the same; and their godly carriage and Christian behavior was such as left a deep impression in the minds of many; and though some few shrunk at these first conflicts and sharp beginnings (as it was no marvel), yet many more came on with fresh courage, and greatly animated others. And, in the end, notwithstanding all these storms of opposition, they all got over at length. Some at one time and some at another, and some in one place and some in another, and met together again according to their desires, with no small rejoicing."

XIII.

PILGRIM LIFE IN AMSTERDAM.

"What brought you hither?" This question with which the emigrant is saluted on his first landing in a strange country, ought to be distinctly answered, however rudely it may be put; at least the voluntary exile should be able to give a reply to his own satisfaction.

Look at the groups of Pilgrims, as they come ashore on the quays of the Low Countries. Rustic, for the most part, in appearance, of different ages, and each carrying some little article of which they are too careful to trust it with the strangers who speak to them in a foreign language. They gaze around them with an air of simple wonder, and the younger Pilgrims are amused and bewildered with the strange looking words painted on the sign-boards. What can people so inexperienced, and of such simple habits, intend to do in a place like this?

They have a reason for coming. They heard that "sundry from London and other parts of the land who had been exiled and persecuted for the same cause, were gone to Holland, and lived at Amsterdam and in other parts of the land, and also that here was freedom of religion "or all men."

Conscience, then, brought them hither. But conscience will not provide for a man's household. Certainly not. Yet where there is an enlightened and good conscience, in other words, rectitude of principle, there is usually found in connection with it soundness of judgment, an average amount of good sense, forethought, and willingness either to labor or to endure, for a worthy object. Look again at this Pilgrim party. There is an air of sobriety about them, a certain kindness, with unmistakable decision, a combination of gentleness and of firmness quite distinctive. They know well that they will have to grapple with difficulties. In the nature of things, it must be a long time before they can accommodate themselves to the customs of the country, and find suitable occupation for their temporal support. Their funds are small, and it is too possible that they will have to suffer from straits, not the less severe, because secretly endured. Bradford says: "They saw many goodly and fortified cities, strongly walled, and guarded with troops of armed men. Also they heard a strange and uncouth language, and beheld the different manners and customs of the people, with their strange fashions and attires; all so far differing from that of their plain country villages, wherein they were bred and born and had so long lived, as it seemed that they were come into a new world. But those were not the things they much looked on, or long took up their thoughts; for they had other work in hand, and another kind of war to wage and maintain. For though they saw fair and beautiful cities, flowing with abundance of all sorts of wealth, yet it was not long before they saw the grim and grizzled face of poverty, coming on them like an armed man, with whom they must buckle and encounter, and from whom they could not fly. But they were armed with faith and patience against him and all his encounters; and though they were sometimes foiled, yet, by God's assistance, they prevailed, and got the victory."

They were favored with leaders of great wisdom and experience. Brewster was perfectly at home in all the scenes around him. In the service of Secretary Davison he had the charge of the keys of one of the Cautionary towns, and he was well acquainted with the ways of the people. Bradford, in the vigor of early manhood, thoughtful, prudent, and active, was ready for any service which might tend to the help and comfort of his brethren; and their pastor, Robinson, as we shall see, was remarkably fitted to be their guide and teacher. True, their reliance was not in the wisdom or in the strength of men, but under God, they valued the gifts and esteemed the persons of those who had been raised up to conduct their affairs.

Their first object after their arrival in Holland was to find a religious home. Naturally they sought out their old friends in Amsterdam. There they met John Smyth, Richard Clifton, Francis Johnson, and Henry Ainsworth, and some who were personally acquainted with the martyrs, Barrowe, Greenwood, and Penry. They soon ascertained, however, that in the Christian society under the care of Smyth, as well as in the first church of the same order, in the city, there were some things likely to disturb their equanimity. The ministry of Francis Johnson was edifying, and they were much impressed by the manner in which he administered Christian ordinances. For Henry Ainsworth they had the highest esteem, yet, as in the church at Corinth, contentions had arisen, and they were unwilling to be identified with a party. For the same reason they hesitated to join the church under the pastorate of Smyth, not to mention some eccentricities of opinion he manifested, on the subject of reading the Scriptures in public, and on other points.

The Pilgrims, after a year's experience, on the whole, decided not to remain at Amsterdam. We may glance, nevertheless, at the order of services as conducted during the time of their brief sojourn.

The morning exercises on the Sabbath began at eight o'clock and continued until twelve.

They commenced with prayer, then read one or two chapters of the Bible, explaining the sense, and held conference together on the subject. The books were then laid aside, and after a second prayer, one of the members preached from a text of Scripture for nearly an hour. A second member followed with another sermon or exhortation of the same duration, succeeded by a third, fourth, or fifth, as time would allow. Finally, the presiding minister or elder offered prayer, and urged the brethren to the exercise of Christian liberality, when a collection was made for the poor, and the meeting was closed with the benediction.

The service in the afternoon began at two o'clock and lasted three or four hours. The exercise of church discipline followed. This was the course for the day in the church connected with John Smyth,— probably there might be a little variation from it in the church of which Francis Johnson and Henry Ainsworth were ministers.

The Pilgrims seem to have lost confidence in the judgment of their old friend and former teacher, John Smyth. Apart from his change of sentiment, in reference to baptism, his views on public worship were afterwards, to say the least, extremely curious and peculiar. There is no reason, however, to question his sincerity, and the services he rendered entitle him to honorable and grateful remembrance. In answer to the charge of vacillation, he says: " I do profess that I will every day, as my errors shall be discovered, confess them and renounce them; for it is our covenant made with God to forsake every evil way, whether in opinion or practice, that shall be manifested unto us at any time, and, therefore, let no man plead now as some have formerly done: ' These men are inconsistent. They would have they know not what, they will never be satisfied,' and the like.

" For we profess even so much as they object, that we are inconstant in error, that we would have the truth, though in many particulars we are ignorant of it. We will never be satisfied in endeavoring to reduce the worship and ministry of the church to the primitive, apostolic institution, from which it as yet is so far distant."

XIV.

THE PILGRIM PASTOR IN LEYDEN.

The Pilgrims removed to the "fair city of Leyden in 1609." No instance of what Dr. Chalmers calls "terrestrial adaptation," could be more remarkable of its kind than the location of Robinson, as the representative and advocate of their principles in this eminent seat of learning. The fame of its university attracted opulent families from various parts of the continent, to secure the advantages of education it afforded. The liberality of the government made it the asylum of Protestant refugees, many of whom were distinguished for their scholastic and theological attainments.

The pastor of the Pilgrims was worthy to take his place among the most illustrious of these philosophers and divines. For a time he had to encounter the prejudice and reserve occasioned by his attachment to the cause of the Separations, but in the exercise of patience and the meekness of wisdom, he found his true position.

Elder Brewster found occupation as a printer. The needful capital for the business was advanced by Mr. Brewer. He "kept no open shop," but supplied books extensively for circulation in England. In addition to his printing establishment, Brewster taught the English language to Danish and German students in the University. Some of the members of the church were weavers; Bradford manufactured silk; others obtained a livelihood by attendance on temporary residents in Leyden, whom they accommodated with suitable apartments. In various ways they obtained a moderate competency, and, by their diligence, kindness, and integrity, gained the confidence of the citizens. On the 5th of May, 1611, Robinson, in conjunction with William Jackson, Henry Wood, and Reynalph Tschickins, purchased a house and garden situated opposite, and to the south of the belfry of St. Peter's church, the oldest church in Leyden.

Here Robinson lived. On the south side of his residence was the Falyde Bagyn church, and next to him was the house of William Symons. In the garden attached to his dwelling, Robinson might be seen in earnest colloquy with Henry Jacob, William Ames, and Robert Parker, Puritan ministers of kindred spirit, who were tending gradually to the principles held by the Pilgrims.

The singular moderation of their pastor, and his

catholicity of spirit won them to the truth, where a teacher of less genial temper might have irritated and repelled. He had evidently profited by the counsels of his venerable tutor at Cambridge, William Perkins.

That Christian Nestor says: "There can be no peace, no Christian neighborhood, no true friendship, unless we bear with one another, and one toward another do carry himself in an even and moderate course.

"It is the property of true love to pass by many wants, and the more that a Christian is rooted in true love, the more infirmities will he pass by in whom he loves. He setteth no limits to himself how many or how long to bear.

"Show thyself that though thou hast been partaker of God's favor, and that thou hast felt in thy soul the sweetness of His mercies, by being mild and merciful to thy brethren, out of that great sea of mercies which God lets flow over thee all thy life long. Let fall some drops of mercy on thy brother."

It is most instructive to observe that the men who proved so inflexible in their adherence to principle, were trained under a ministry richly imbued with the spirit of charity. They were impressed deeply with the apostolic lesson: "Though I give my body to be burned, and have not charity, it profiteth me nothing."

We may judge from the sententious style of his writings, in what manner Robinson would counsel the brethren who sought his advice in the various perplexities and difficulties of life.

He would have them in all things to act with *equability aud moderation.* " There are some," he says, " of that boisterous and tempestuous disposition, that they can do nothing calmly or a little; their unruly affections, which should follow after leisurely, do force on so violently their understanding, will, and whole man, as there is no stay with them; but in all their notions they are like unto those beasts which, for the unequal length of their hinder legs, cannot possibly go but by leaps. Such a stormy nature, with a very little zeal amongst, may make a great stir in the world, but is justly to be suspected."

Speaking of a *modest and temperate spirit*, he says: " Peter and John, with the other apostles, prayed to the Lord for boldness in the speaking of his word, Acts iv. 29. Many others also pray for boldness, as they did; but forget that they are not apostles, nor infallibly directed, as they were. Who, if they knew themselves aright, and how prone they are to speak their own word instead of God's, would rather pray for modesty and advisedness, that they rush not upon the rock of error. Besides, they so prayed in regard of the threatenings of unbelievers with whom they had to do. But amongst brethren and Christians, let us rather affect the lamb's bleat than the lion's roar."

Of *truth, and the manner in which it should be maintained*, he writes: " All truth, by whomsoever spoken, is of God. This truth is always the same whilst the God of truth is in heaven, what entertainment soever it find with men upon earth; it is always praiseworthy, though no man praise it; and hath no reason, or just cause to be ashamed, though it often goes with a scratched face.

" We must love and attain to the knowledge of the truth in ourselves first; lest we be clouds without rain, promising that to others which we ourselves want; and must, in our places, afterwards make manifestation and profession of it.

" All truth is not to be spoken at all times. 'A fool uttereth all his mind; but a wise man keeps it in for afterwards,' Prov. xxix. 11, yet nothing not true at any time, or for any cause. He that hath but a right philosophical spirit, and is but morally honest, would rather suffer many deaths, than call a pin a point, or speak the least thing against his understanding or persuasion.

" A man in pleading for the truth may show his judgment and understanding best in the matter;

but his grace and godliness in the manner, when he handles a good cause well, and the Lord's cause after the Lord's manner. Sometimes men pretend God's truth and zeal for it, when indeed they make their pleas for truth serve only for hackneys, for their lusts to ride on whither they would have them; sometimes men seriously intend truth, and yet mingle, both with their good intention, and, it may be, true assertion also, such their personal conceptions and distempers, as Christ loseth more by their inordinateness that way than he gains both by their sound knowledge and fervent zeal of and for His truth."

In this pointed and forcible manner he gave utterance to maxims of the soundest wisdom. No member of his flock could walk with him five minutes in his garden, or meet him in conference at his house, without receiving lessons worth remembering, and given with such homely illustrations that he could not fail to understand their meaning.

Take another illustration: "The safest way not to be deceived by others, specially to our spiritual prejudice, is not to deceive ourselves; which till we do, no other can deceive us. Hence is it, that God in His word so often warns us, that we be not deceived, and that we deceive not ourselves and our own souls. But, and if we either put out our own eyes with our finger, through passion or prejudice, or willingly wink at dangers which we might foresee, who will pity us, if we fall into the ditch of deceit which others dig for us."

The church regarded their pastor with affection, based on esteem for his worth, and combined with a grateful sense of the benefit derived from his example and his teaching. Robinson fully reciprocated their attachment. In reply to Bernard who spoke contemptuously of the exercise of church rights by such members as " Simon the saddler, Tomkin the tailor, and Billy the bellows-maker," Robinson gives this testimony respecting the church at Leyden:

" If ever I saw the beauty of Zion, and the glory of the Lord filling his tabernacle, it hath been in the manifestation of the divers graces of God in the church, in that heavenly harmony, and comely order, wherein by the grace of God we are set and walk; wherein if your eyes had but seen the brethren's sober and modest carriage one toward another, their humble and willing submission unto their guides in the Lord, their tender compassion toward the weak, their fervent zeal against scandalous offenders, and their long suffering toward all, you would, I am persuaded, change your mind, and be compelled to take up your parable, and bless where you purposed to curse, as Balaam did, Numbers xxiii. But whatsoever you, and all others do, these our experimental comforts, neither you nor any shall take from us."

It was not permitted to the pastor of the church in Leyden to pursue the even tenor of his way, caring only for the welfare of his flock, and laboring with them to advance the kingdom of Christ. He was bitterly assailed by the clergy of the English establishment. They had no just occasion for the rancorous hostility they still manifested.

Robinson cherished true kindness of spirit toward his Christian brethren who continued in the Church of England. " For myself, he says, " thus I believe with my heart before God, and profess with my tongue, and leave before the world, that I have one and the same faith, hope, spirit, baptism, and Lord, which I had in the church of England, and none other; that I esteem so many in that church, of what state, or order soever, as are truly partakers of that faith, as I account many thousands to be, for my Christian brethren, and myself a fellow-member with them of that one mystical body of Christ, scattered far and wide throughout the world; that I have always, in spirit and affection, all Christian fellowship and communion with them, and am most ready, in all outward actions and exercises of religion, lawful and lawfully done, to express the same.

" I cannot communicate with, or submit unto the church order and ordinances there established, either in state or act, without being condemned of mine own heart, and therein provoking God, who is greater than my heart, to condemn me much more."

Conscience, and not faction, led to his separation, and he was anxious that in his withdrawal there should be nothing to alienate him from any who loved the Lord Jesus Christ in sincerity. "As they that affect alienation from others," he says, "make their differences as great, and the adverse opinion or practice as odious as they can, thereby to further their desired victory over them, and to harden themselves and their side against them, so, on the contrary, they who desire peace and accord, both interpret things in the best part they reasonably can, and seek how and where they may find any lawful door of entry into accord and agreement with others; of which latter member, I profess myself (by the grace of God) both a companion and a guide; especially in regard of my Christian countrymen, to whom God hath tied me by so many inviolable bonds; accounting it a cross that I am, in any particular, compelled to dissent from them; but a benefit, and matter of rejoicing, when I can in anything with good conscience unite with them in matter, if not in manner, or, where it may be, in both. And this affection, the Lord and my conscience are my witnesses, I have always nourished in my breast, even when I seemed furthest drawn from them; and so all that have a true knowledge of my course can testify with me, and how I have still opposed in others, and repressed in mine own people, to my power, all sour zeal against, and peremptory rejection of such as, whose holy graces challenge better use and respect from all Christians."

Robinson had no love for controversy. "Disputations in religion," he observes, "are sometimes necessary, but always dangerous; drawing the best spirits into the head from the heart, and leaving it either empty of all, or too full of fleshly zeal and passion; if extraordinary care be not taken still to supply, and fill it anew with pious affections toward God and loving toward men."

"As for myself," he says, "I could much rather have desired to have built up myself and the poor flock over which the Holy Ghost hath set me in holy peace, as becometh the house of God, 'wherein no sound of axe or hammer or other tool of iron is to be heard,' 1 King vi. 7, than to enter the lists of contention."

But he had no alternative as set for the defence of the truth. He was not however to be drawn into personalities. Joseph Hall indulged in the bitterest vituperation. Robinson, in reply, said, "I will be nothing less in contention, but will count it a victory to be overcome in odious provocations and reproaches."

"Your system is one of novelty," said one of his

opponents. Robinson answered: "The things we teach are not new, but old truths renewed; so are we no less persuaded, that the church constitution in which we are set is cast in the apostolical and primitive mould, and not one day nor one hour younger, in the nature and form of it, than the first church of the New Testament."

"But you make no progress," rejoined the other; "you have no proof arising from the 'increase of God.'"

"Indeed," replied Robinson, "the church of England hath the advantage of us; and, as I suppose, of all the churches in the world for monstrous speedy growth and increase. It grew from top to toe unto a true and entire body of a sudden, and before the greatest part of it so much as heard the gospel preached in any measure for their conversion. . . . Let it be so, that the cause of religion is to be measured by the multitude of them that profess it; yet must it further be considered that religion is not always sown and reaped in one age. 'One soweth and another reapeth.' John iv. 37. John Huss and Jerome of Prague finished their testimony, in Bohemia and at Constance, a hundred years before Luther; and Wickliffe in England wellnigh as long before them, and yet neither the one nor the other with the like success unto Luther.

"And the many that are already gathered by the

mercy of God into the kingdom of His son Jesus, and the nearness of many more through the whole land, for the regions are white unto harvest, do promise within less than an hundred years, if our sins and theirs make not us and them unworthy of this mercy, a very plenteous harvest.

"That we have been, here and there, up and down, without sure footing, is our portion in this present evil world, common to us with the more worthy servants of God going before us, who have wandered in wildernesses and mountains, and dens and caves of the earth." Heb. xi. 38.

Every point of objection to the principles and practices of the voluntary church under his care, Robinson met with a felicity of expression and force of reasoning that invest his writings with a charm, to the ecclesiastical student, not lost after the lapse of two centuries and a half.

Whilst occupied in preparing these treatises and in the duties of his pastorate, he took part in public discussions in connection with the chief men of the University. He derived valuable hints for the guidance of the Pilgrims in civil matters, from the lectures of the professors, and turned every thing in his position and association to the advantage of the cause with which he was so closely identified.

Well might the church "esteem him very highly in love." "He was not easily to be paralleled," they tell us, "for all things. Never people upon earth lived more lovingly together than we, the church at Leyden did." Nor was this testimony borne by his own people and immediate friends alone.

Hoornbeck says, "John Robinson was most dear to us while he lived, was on familiar terms with the Leyden theologians, and was greatly esteemed by them."

Even Baylie, the fiery polemic most opposed to the principles of the Pilgrims, is constrained to admit that "Robinson was a man of excellent parts, and the most learned, polished, and modest spirit that ever separated from the church of England."

XV.

SECOND PILGRIM CHURCH. — HENRY JACOB.

THE question of " flight in persecution " was often discussed in the times of the Reformation. Some of the most eloquent letters of Calvin were written on this subject, and his counsels were substantially the same with those given by Robinson at a later period. The opinion, however, was strongly expressed by some of the brethren in London, that the position taken by the Pilgrims, as exiles, was not worthy of the cause to which they were devoted.

In a dialogue between a " Christian " and an " antichristian," in which an " impartial man " takes part (1615), the following passages occur :

I. " One thing there is yet which hath much troubled me and others, and, in my judgment, hath much hindered the growth of godliness in this kingdom, and that is, that many, as soon as they see or fear trouble will ensue, they fly into another nation who cannot see their conversation, and thereby deprive many poor ignorant souls in their own nation of their reformation and of their conversation amongst them."

C. " Oh! that hath been the overthrow of religion in this land; the best able and greater part being gone, and leaving behind some few, who, by the others' departure, have had their afflictions and contempt increased, which hath been the cause of many falling back, and of the adversaries' exulting. But they will tell us, we are not to judge things by the effects, therefore we must prove that their flight be unlawful, or we say nothing.

"And first, whereas it is said by some of the fliers, that many of the people of God fled into foreign countries, and that God gave approbation thereof, as Moses, David, our Saviour Christ in his infancy, and others, thinking thereby to justify this their flight; I answer, God preserved Moses and the rest in their flight, till the time was come that he employed them in his service, then in no case would He suffer them to fly; as when Moses manifested his exceeding backwardness to the Lord's work, in helping his people out of bondage, using many excuses, the Lord was very angry with him. And whither did our Saviour fly when the time came that he was to ' show himself to Israel.' If any of these men can prove the Lord requireth no work at their hands to be done for his glory and the salvation of thousands of ignorant souls in their own nation, let them stay in foreign countries.

" But I trust God's people have learned not to say, the time is not yet come that Babel should be destroyed and the Lord's house builded.

" Did God respect his work and people, that all must put to their helping hand, and none must withdraw their shoulder lest others were discouraged; and is there no regard to be had thereof now, but any occasion, as fear of a little imprisonment or the like, may excuse any, both from the Lord's work and the help of their brethren, that for want of their society and comfort are exceedingly weakened, if not overcome. If answer be made, they perform their duty in both, that they do the Lord's work, the pastor feeding his flock, and the people walking in fellowship one toward another; I demand, doth the Lord require no more work of them? doth he not require that they should help to cast down Babel? If reply be made, they do it by their books; I answer, that may be done, and their lights shine by their mouths and conversations among the wicked, which is the greatest means of converting them and destroying antichrist's kingdom : ' They overcame,' not by flying away, but by the blood of the Lamb, and by the word of their testimony; and they loved not their lives unto the death.

" God's people are the light of the world, a city set

on a hill, a candle set on the candlestick, giving light to all that come in, and therefore must shine by their persons more than by their books. And great help and encouragement would it be to God's people, in affliction of imprisonment and the like, to have their brethren's presence to administer to their souls or bodies.'

Robinson justified the course of his brethren; " As we shall perceive either our flying or abiding," he says, " to be meet for God's glory and the good of men, especially of our family and those nearest to us; and for our furtherance in holiness; and as we have strength to wade through the dangers of persecution, so we are with good conscience to use the one or other; which, our hope and comfort also are, we have done in these our days of sorrow ; some of us coming over by banishment, and others otherwise.'

In truth, there was little choice between a state of banishment, and the troubles to be endured in their native land. Many of the Pilgrims began to feel the yearnings so natural to the exile. Francis Johnson addressed a petition about this time to King James, in which he prays, " that it would please him, now, after our long exile and other manifold afflictions, to vouchsafe us that gracious sufferance that we may be permitted to live in peace, under His Majesty's government, in our native country;

there to observe all the ordinances of Christ given to his church, without being urged to the use or approbation of any remnants of the apostasy of antichrist, or other human traditions whatsoever."

Henry Jacob does not appear to have entered into the discussion, as to the course of a Christian in these circumstances, but it is probable that it had its practical effect upon his own mind. However this may be, he returned from Holland to London very shortly after this agitation of the question.

There was still a "remnant" left of the faithful brethren after the martyrdom of Barrowe, Greenwood, and Penry. Severe measures of repression were adopted by the authorities to prevent the possibility of their resuscitation. All who were known to have expressed sympathy with them were called to account.

The following record illustrates the extreme lengths to which the authorities were determined to go. "In June, 1594, Mr. John Clerk the elder, late mayor of St. Albans, was brought into the high commission court, where, among other articles, these were objected to him: That you the said John Clerk, in the year 1593, permitted divers and sundry ministers, not licensed or allowed by authority, to be privately exercised in your own house, and namely, one John Penry, lately executed; or, at least, have secretly received and entertained the said Penry, and have had much conference with him within your own house, and have uttered your liking of many of his factious opinions, inasmuch that you have kept many of his seditious books, supposed to be written by him, and have dispersed or imparted some of them to others; then, that the said Penry not long before his arraignment was at your house, and had conference with you, and that before his departure from you, understanding that he was endangered, did *there promise to pray for him*, saying that you hoped both he and his cause should return with credit." *

It was supposed that by these means the church was extirpated. "As for those we call Brownists," said Lord Bacon, "being, when they were at the most, a very small number of very silly and base people, here and there in corners dispersed, they are now, thanks be to God, by the good remedies that have been used, suppressed and worn out, so as there is scarce any news of them."

The vine was indeed almost torn up by the roots. Its branches were broken down, and lay bleeding on the ground, to be trampled upon by every passer-by; but a slender stem remained in which there was vitality no power on earth was suffered to destroy. In other words, the church of the Separatists, though,

* Lansdowne MSS., 982, 89.

to a great extent, scattered and peeled, did not become quite extinct in London. The rays of light by which to trace its existence are extremely faint, but, from incidental notices, we find that though " cast down," it was not destroyed.

On the 21st October, 1608, I. Chamberlain writes to Dudley Carleton to tell him that "there was a nest or assembly of Brownists discovered on Sunday about Finsbury, whereof five or six and thirty were apprehended with their preacher, that use to exercise at Christ church (Southwark)."

Henry Jacob was in communication with people so designated. Writing to his "Christian and beloved friends in London and elsewhere," July 18, 1612, he says: "The great afflictions which it hath pleased God to call me unto, only for testifying His heavenly truth against the grievous corruptions of the church in our land, are well known unto you all, my most dear and loving friends. In the midst of which my troubles, what comfort I have received from you, though I publish not, yet hath a most thankful remembrance thereof remained in my heart, and with God a most precious recompense is laid up for you at the last day."

With manifest desire to follow the truth and to fulfil the trust implied in its honest reception, Henry Jacob proceeded on his return from Holland, in 1616, with his wonted diffidence and caution. He had been restrained from committing himself to the Separatists, from deference to his friends of the Puritan party. They were now fully convinced that the expectation of further reformation, with the royal sanction, could no longer be retained. Arthur Hildersham, the patriarchal leader of the Puritans at this time, had been thrown into prison, and two of his congregation were committed to the King's Bench in Southwark. Here, and almost within sight of the Clink prison in which Francis Johnson, his former antagonist, had been immured, Jacob proposed to collect the flock which had been dispersed in the " cloudy and dark day."

He expressed the opinion that a church ought to meet statedly in one place, and there to maintain public worship and to give its testimony. " Which also," he says, " we may likewise affirm of the church of Antioch, 1 Cor. xiv. 23; Acts xiv. 27; Acts xv. 12, 25; Acts xx. 28, and of Rome, and of Jerusalem, and of Ephesus, etc., in those days. For though these cities were great and populous, yet being unbelieving and hateful enemies to the gospel, each of them had then of faithful Christians but one particular constant congregation only. Like as the Protestants are in the cities at this day under the Spanish King; or as they were in divers cities of France before the peace was made, and as we were in London in Queen Mary's time. Where yet we deny not, that then some particular congregations being (as that of Jerusalem was before) greater than other some, did, by reason of persecution, meet occasionally and uncertainly in divers smaller numbers. But these smaller numbers were not so many churches properly, because they were uncertain and occasional, — a true and proper church being always necessarily an ordinary set company and a constant society."

In these views Arthur Hildersham, Job Throgmorton, Richard Maunsel, and the venerable John Dod, so far acquiesced, as to express their approbation of the purpose of Henry Jacob to form such a church or " constant society."

Accordingly he convened several of the brethren together, — Staresmore, Browne, Prior, Almey, Throughton, Allen, Gilbert, Farre, Goodal, and others.

He explained to them the nature of a Christian church. " A true, visible, and ministerial church of Christ," he said, " is a number of faithful people formed by their willing consent in a spiritual outward society, or body-politic, ordinarily meeting in one place; instituted by Christ in his New Testament, and having the power to exercise ecclesiastical government and all God's other spiritual ordinances — the means of salvation, — in and for itself immediately from Christ."

A day of solemn fasting and prayer was appointed, and, at the close of the exercises of devotion, each of the brethren made open confession of his faith in our Lord Jesus Christ; and then, standing together, they joined hands and solemnly covenanted with each other in the presence of Almighty God, to walk together in all God's ways and ordinances, according as he had already revealed, or should further make known unto them." Mr. Jacob was then chosen their pastor by the suffrage of the brotherhood, and others were appointed to the office of deacons, with fasting and prayer and imposition of hands.

The newly organized church issued a manifesto in defence of the position they had taken as a Christian society.

"Touching the necessity that lieth upon us, to obey Christ rather than man, in our using of the true and in refusing the contrary ecclesiastical ordinances: we believe that, by the word of God, all Christians are bound, each for his own part, to keep and observe, actually and perpetually, the affirmative ecclesiastical commandments and ordinances in the gospel, as well as the negative; that is, so far as one person sufficeth to perform the same, singly and by himself, he ought so to do; and where some number are required, and are ready, for the observing of any such commandment, there each

Christian which can be present with other, standeth bound to give his consent, and to make one with them therein; always after the best order they can, and namely, that main order which is in the gospel, notwithstanding whatsoever man's forbidding, or whatsoever affliction in the world shall follow upon it.

"This direct and ordinary means of hope and faith, of grace and salvation, we ought to prefer before our life." "We are clearly commanded to obey God rather than man. And God commanding us to fear, and to love, and to serve Him; he commandeth us the necessary means and ways of doing so, even that church in and by which, ordinarily, we must do so, that we may be accepted; which, under the gospel, is such a free congregation.

"Where we see that this only is now Christ's true, visible church; and no other form of a visible church is; wherefore, we are all bound, with all care, to hearken to the express precept of the Holy Ghost concerning this point, saying, 'This is the way, walk ye in it;' which also the harmony of confessions, teacheth; namely, this we ought to do, notwithstanding men of power and might shall say nay.

"Now, therefore, we demand, and do most earnestly crave of every impartial Christian to answer us. What false things have we here affirmed? What, on our part, is evil? What is wicked in all this? If nothing, as we are firmly persuaded in our souls that there is nothing, then we pray and earnestly entreat, in the bowels of mercy in Jesus Christ, every one to pardon our consciences in that, thus doing, we stand to give actual obedience to our heavenly Lord and Saviour in his own commandments and ordinances; which also we do, that we may thereby, as by the only true complete means, get assurance of salvation to our souls, which otherwise we, for our parts, cannot find."

In an address to the king, they very justly reminded His Majesty that their "meeting thus, only in a competent congregation," could not "in any way in the least measure be prejudicial or suspicious to His Highness' peace or dignity."

There is something, when all the circumstances of the case are considered, very noble in this calm and equable resolve of Henry Jacob. He was evidently a man of pacific temper, and perhaps constitutionally timid. But his allegiance to truth, on that account, was the more striking. Steadily he advanced to the point to which he was conducted by the pure light which shone upon him in weakness, privation, and suffering. The church he planted, or rather reorganized in Southwark, exists to this day. Standing in the direct line from him in the pastorate, the writer of these lines craves the indulgence of the reader, to render a tribute to his memory, though it may slightly interrupt the course of the narrative. The continuous history of the church has yet to be written. Henry Jacob remained at his post eight years, and was followed in turn by John Lothrop. Both went to America and there died. Of the place in which Jacob located himself, or where he was buried, we have no knowledge.

It is gratifying to discover the traces, however faint, of those who have advanced in the fore rank in the cause of truth and freedom. But the thought is not without interest, that an entire continent may be regarded as a place of sepulchre for one whose principles gave birth to the nation by which it is peopled.

The modesty of Henry Jacob was as remarkable as his zeal and devotedness. "The Lord, I doubt not, will raise up others," he said, "that shall more effectually bear witness unto this truth in due time; even until the toleration hereof in England. Being with much vehemency charged, that for no just cause I have refused to conform to the church order in England, I could therefore do no less but give out, yea, unto *posterity*, the true and most important reasons of my dissenting herein." *

* It was the lesson given by the example of the pastor of the church, in 1616, that impressed the mind of the present pastor with the sense of sacred obligation, to seek the perpetuity of the church under circumstances as trying to faith and patience, as can well be imagined in modern times. The old meeting-house (in a most obscure and forbidding spot in Union street, Southwark) was lost to the society. For three years the church could find no settled abode or any site of ground for building. In that interval of trial and of weakness, the most determined and persevering attempt was made to defeat the object. But the faithful few held on until a place was secured on which to build the "Memorial Church."

A more simple, persevering effort for a good object was never made, than that of the poor members, who had little to oppose to the injuries they suffered, but prayers and tears. They were not overcome. The visit made by the pastor in 1859 to America, though it failed to realize the amount necessary to complete the memorial design,— yet saved the church, and preserved the property from alienation. Without the kind and spontaneous aid rendered by the descendants of the Pilgrims, it is not too much to say, that the church must have succumbed beneath a pressure, the nature and severity of which the world will never know. The writer would have been almost content that he should have found a grave himself in the land which contains the remains of Henry Jacob and of John Lothrop, so that England might have witnessed the spontaneous and successful effort of the descendants of the Pilgrims in America to complete this memorial. As it is, the finger of those who still mock at the design, as Utopian, is pointed at the fragmental building as a failure. But the day will yet come when the work shall be accomplished, and the contempt of the proud will be exchanged for admiration at a peaceful and yet glorious demonstration, too significant to be mistaken. Let every reader of these lines say: "I will have a stone in that building," and send the tribute by the first post to Mr. W. G. Lambert, 43 Broadway, New York, or to Mr. James Lawrence, Milk Street, Boston, Massachusetts.

XVI.

DISCUSSIONS ON LEAVING HOLLAND.

WE resume the story. The words of Robinson quoted in the former chapter, "As we shall perceive either our flying or abiding to meet for God's glory and the good of men, especially of *our family* and *those nearest to us;* and for our furtherance in holiness; and as we have strength to wade through the dangers of persecutions, so we are with good conscience to use one or other;" no doubt afford the clue to the movement of the Pilgrims in preparing to return from Holland. In their plans and arrangements they had special regard to the best interests of their children, in connection with the opportunities they might have for promoting the cause of truth. Bradford, with his usual clearness and simplicity, has told us the reasons that led to the consideration of the question of removal. But besides the causes assigned by him, we find that influences were at work to abridge their means of Christian usefulness, that must have added force to their determination to seek another place of settlement.

King James was so absorbed in the discussions which led to the Synod of Dort, that his attention for a time seems to have been diverted from the operations carried on by the Pilgrim leaders. The royal polemic wrote letters in French to the States-General calculated, as he vainly imagined, to settle all the questions in dispute. His self-complacency seems to have rendered him insensible in his domestic relations. On the day of the queen's funeral, the returned messenger from Holland tells us, "he had a most convenient occasion to get presence of His Majesty at Greenwich," because of the funeral in London, "there were none at court but the king and my lord admiral. His Majesty, so far from yielding to grief on the occasion, was only inquisitive to know, from the gossiping envoy, in what estimation his theological epistles were held by the divines and the court of Holland."

"He was much displeased," that more prominent mention had not been made of his name, for he considered himself the principal hero in the contest.

The king, prompted by the bishops, as soon as he was apprised of the efforts made by Robinson and Brewster to diffuse their principles, devised means for their repression.

The light which shone from Leyden was too

effulgent for the defenders of prelacy, and no pains were spared that it might be quenched.

The Pilgrims marked the course of events, and anticipated the dangers by which their cause was threatened.

Holland had never been considered by them as their proper home. They were Englishmen. They loved the language of their country, they were addicted to its usages, and it was contrary to their most cherished predilections that their descendants should be merged in the Dutch nation. They were moreover Protestant Christians, of the class who had been taught to keep holy the Sabbath and to value its ordinances. In this respect their views were greatly in advance of those maintained by the continental reformers, and it grieved them that their children should witness the scenes of revelry that were so common in Holland. Notwithstanding their parental care and consistent example, they observed, with deep and growing anxiety, that the youth of their company, in instances far too frequent, yielded to the influences around them, and became inoculated with the military spirit of the times and the love of foreign adventure. Besides all this, they found many of the English exiles were bent on returning to their own country, and that others would be tempted either to compromise or to conceal their principles, in order to live in the land of their fathers' sepulchres.

Yet in the contemplated change they did not act precipitately. The more thoughtful and experienced held private conferences. We may see them in the arbor in the pastor's garden. The children of Robinson,— John, Bridget, Isaac, Mercy, Favor, and Jacob, — wonder what is the topic of such close and earnest conversation between their father, Elder Brewster, John Carver, Robert Cushman, and William Bradford. Books of voyages are consulted. They are well versed in the history of the " Travels, Adventures, and Observations of Captain John Smith," Harcourt's Voyage to Guiana, the works of Sir Walter Raleigh and of Hakluyt. They learn from the Huguenot refugees in Leyden the plans of colonization projected by De Monts. The discoveries of Henry Hudson excite great interest. In 1607, after taking the sacrament with his crew at the little church of Ethelburga, in Bishopsgate, London, he commenced his voyages. In his third voyage, which he undertook in the employ of the Dutch, he discovered the river called by his name. His journal is now before the leaders of the Pilgrims. He says: " The land is the finest for cultivation that I ever in my life set foot upon, and it also abounds in trees of every description." " The natives are a very good people. The climate," he adds, " is not bad, though sometimes colder than is pleasant." A trading station has just been established by the Dutch merchants at Manhattan, at the entrance to the river. There is, then, the prospect of securing a settlement in the western world if the path be made plain by the hand of Providence. They unite in prayer for divine direction, and it is determined to submit the subject to the consideration of the church. Maria Hardy, the maid-servant, opens the gate for the elder and his friends, who ponder in their hearts the weighty matter on their way home. They felt the seriousness of the business, and were alive to the difficulties involved in the projected undertaking, but they were animated by " the hope and inward zeal of laying some good foundation, or at least to make some way thereunto, for the propagating and advancing the gospel of the kingdom of Christ in these remote parts of the world; yea, though they should be but as stepping-stones unto others for performing of so great a work."

The proposition to remove to America, on being made public, " raised many variable opinions." They did not conceal from the brethren the dangers of the expedition. The fatigue, privation, and exposure to the perils by sea, and by land, were depicted to them in the most vivid manner by those who objected to the enterprise. They described with horrible minuteness the practices of cannibalism, and showed what kind of death might be expected in the hands of cruel, barbarous, and treacherous savages. We can scarcely wonder that, in hearing these recitals, the timid began to quake and tremble. Besides, it was represented that a colony could not be planted with greater sums of money than their estates would command. It so happened, moreover, that the attempt made to make a plantation at Sagadahoc, though sanctioned and supported by men of wealth and influence in England, had resulted in the most disastrous failure. All these things were distinctly before the minds of the Pilgrims at the outset. Deliberately they counted the cost.

"It was answered, that all great and honorable actions were accompanied with great difficulties, and must be both enterprised and overcome with answerable courage. It was granted the dangers were great, but not desperate, and the difficulties were many, but not invincible; for although there were many of them likely, yet were they not certain."

It might be that some of the things feared might never befall them; others, by providence, care, and the use of good means, might in a great measure be prevented; and all of them, through the help of God, by fortitude and patience, might either be borne or overcome. True it was that such attempts were not to be made and undertaken but upon good ground and reason, not rashly or lightly, as many have done for curiosity, or hope of gain, etc. But their condition was not ordinary, their ends were good and honorable, their calling lawful and urgent, and therefore they might expect a blessing of God in their proceeding; yea, although they should lose their lives in this action, yet they might have comfort in the same; and their endeavors would be honorable. They lived here but as men in exile and in a poor condition; and as great miseries might possibly befall them in this place; for the twelve years of truce were now out, and there was nothing but beating of drums and preparing for war, the events whereof are always uncertain. The Spaniard might prove as cruel as the savages of America, and the famine and pestilence are sore here as there, and liberty less to look out for remedy.

" After many other particular things answered and alleged on both sides, it was fully concluded by the major part to put this design in execution, and to prosecute it by the best means they could."

They reasoned justly as to the probabilities of war between the Dutch and Spaniards. After an interval of twelve years' peace — the time the Pilgrims sojourned in Holland — hostilities recommenced.

The Pilgrims held a consultation as to the most suitable place to " pitch upon, and prepare for."

Some proposed Guiana, but it was thought that country was rather too hot, and, if prosperous, they would be molested by the zealous Spaniard. Unlike the martyr church in London of 1593, they had no desire to keep a frontier line against the power of Spain. Virginia was mentioned, but it was objected that if they were too near the English who were settled there, they might be more exposed to persecution even than in England, and if too far off, they should neither have succor nor defence from them. Finally, it was resolved " to live as a distinct body by themselves, under the general government of Virginia; and by their friends to sue to His Majesty that he would be pleased to grant them *freedom of religion.*

XVII.

NEGOTIATIONS AND CONCLUSIONS CONCERNING VIRGINIA.

In the autumn of 1617, Robert Cushman and John Carver were deputed to negotiate with the Virginia company, and "to procure a patent with as good and ample conditions as they might by any good means obtain."

They took with them the following document, for the satisfaction of the council, to indicate how far they could advance, in terms of peace, consistently with their non-conformist principles.

"Seven articles which the church of Leyden sent to the council of England, to be considered of in respect of their judgments occasioned about their going to Virginia:"

1. To the confession of faith published in the name of the church of England, and to every article thereof we do, with the reformed churches where we live, and also elsewhere, assent wholly.

2. As we do acknowledge the doctrine of faith there taught, so do we the fruits and effects of the

same doctrine, to the begetting of saving faith in thousands in the land (conformists and reformists), as they are called, with whom also, as with our brethren, we do desire to keep spiritual communion in peace, and will practise in our parts all lawful things.

3. The king's majesty we acknowledge for supreme governor in his dominion, in all causes and over all persons, and that none may declare or appeal from his authority or judgment in any cause whatsoever, but that in all things obedience is due unto him, either active, if the thing commanded be not against God's word, or passive if it be, except pardon can be obtained.

4. We judge it lawful for His Majesty to appoint bishops, civil overseers, or officers in authority under him, in the several provinces, dioceses, congregations, or parishes, to oversee the churches, and govern them civilly, according to the laws of the land, unto whom they are in all things to give an account, and by them to be ordered according to godliness.

5. The authority of the present bishops in the land we do acknowledge, so far forth as the same is indeed derived from His Majesty unto them, and as they proceed in his name, whom we will also therein honor in all things, and him in them.

6. We believe that no synod, classes, convocation, or assembly of ecclesiastical officers hath any power

or authority at all, but as the same by the magistrate given unto them.

7. Lastly, we desire to give unto all superiors due honor to preserve the unity of the spirit with all that fear God, to have peace with all men, what in us lieth, and wherein we err to be instructed by any. Subscribed by

JOHN ROBINSON,*
and
WILLIAM BREWSTER.

The messengers of the church in Leyden were not altogether strangers in London. Robinson acknowledged the Christian society under the pastoral care of Henry Jacob, as a "true church," and they received, on their arrival, Christian sympathy from its members and cordial coöperation. Sabin Staresmore in particular, offered his zealous services.

Samuel Fuller, Isaac Allerton, Degory Priest, Edward Winslow, and Sarah Vincent, are described in the records of Leyden as from London. Edward Southworth, whose widow, Alice, was afterwards married to Governor Bradford, lived at Heneage house in Duke's place.

It is probable, therefore, that amongst friends and

---

* This document, which is in the state paper, unfortunately is only a copy. Not a fragment of Robinson's handwriting is known to be in existence.

relatives of the Pilgrims, Carver and Cushman might find a home. Cushman himself went from Canterbury to Leyden, and, in the intervals of business, he "went down," he tells us, "into Kent."

In their visits the negotiators do not appear to have made any encouraging progress in their business.

Willing as the representatives of the church at Leyden were to make all possible concessions for peace, and in the spirit of loyalty, they did not conceal their views of church government. In a letter to Sir John Worstenholme, dated Leyden, January 27, 1617–18, one of the principal members of the Virginia company, they offered some explanations on points specified by the privy council, and on which unjust insinuations had been made against them.

They stated that, in general, there was a resemblance in the order of their church with that of the French reformed churches, whilst they varied in some respects. Sabine Staresmore presented the letter personally to Sir John Worstenholme, and reported the result of the interview (Feb. 14, 1617–18). As the worthy knight read the document, he said, in a tone somewhat impatient: "Who shall make them?"

The question had reference to the appointment of ministers. Staresmore replied, that the power of making was in the church, to be ordained by the imposition of hands, by the fittest instruments they had. " It must be either be in the church," he added, " or from the pope ; and the pope is antichrist." This was strange doctrine to the ears of Sir John, and rather dangerous to broach under the circumstances. " Ho!" said he, " what the pope holds good (as in the Trinity), that we do well to assent to ; but we will not enter into the dispute now. As for these letters I would not show them at any hand lest I should spoil all. I expected these Leyden people would have been of the same mind with the archbishop as to the calling of ministers." Staresmore had no wish to enter further into the subject, and asked Sir John if he had any " very good news, for both the king's majesty and the bishops have consented. I will go to Mr. Chancellor, Sir Talke Greville to-day, and next week you shall hear more."

After long suspense and great discouragements, those who are seeking to gain an important point, often mistake the first appearance of success for complete triumph over their difficulties.

Cushman and Carver found a valuable and steady friend in Sir Edwin Sandys, the son of the archbishop of York, who held Scrooby Manor.

Sir Edwin, writing to Robinson and Brewster from London, November 12, 1617, gives a favorable testimony to the ability and discretion of Cushman and Carver, on their return to Leyden, though the expectations of the brethren there were not realized.

Deacon Carver returned to London in the following month, bearing a letter from Robinson and Brewster to Sir Edwin Sandys, in which, after thankful acknowledgments of his "singular love," expressed in his "great care and earnest endeavor for their good," they state that under God, "above all persons and things in the world," they rely upon him. For his "encouragement in the work," they mention "these instances of inducement."

"1. We verily believe and trust the Lord is with us, unto whom and whose service we have given ourselves in many trials; and that He will graciously prosper our endeavors according to the simplicity of our hearts therein.

"2. We are well weaned from the delicate milk of our mother country, and enured to the difficulties of a strange and hard land, which yet, in a great part, we have by patience overcome.

"3. The people are, for the body of them, industrious and frugal, we think we may safely say, as any company of people in the world.

"4. We are knit together as a body, in a most strict and sacred bond and covenant of the Lord, of violation whereof we make great conscience, and by virtue whereof we hold ourselves strictly tied to all care of each other's good, and of the whole by every one, and so mutually.

"5. Lastly, it is not with us as with other men, whom small things can discourage, or small discontentments cause to wish themselves at home again. We know our entertainment in England and in Holland; we shall much prejudice both our hearts and means by removal; who, if we should be driven to return, we should not hope to recover our present help and comforts, neither indeed look ever, for ourselves, to attain unto the like in any other place during our lives, which are now drawing toward their periods."

"These motives," they add, "we have been bold to tender unto you, which you in your wisdom may also impart to any other of our worshipful friends of the Council with you; of all whose godly disposition and loving toward our despised persons, we are most glad, and shall not fail, by all good means, to continue and increase the same."

We know little of the course of the negotiators from Leyden in their second visit to London. They were "much hindered" and discouraged. The consent given by the bishops to their enterprise must have been nominal, or, at least, they were unwilling that those who were interested should meet to seek the divine blessing. From a letter written under great affliction from the prison in Wood street, by Sabine Staresmore, we learn that he and several brethren in London met with Richard Masterson, a member of the church at Leyden, and others for fasting and prayer. The meeting was discovered. Staresmore and Mr. Blackwell from Amsterdam were taken prisoners. To screen himself, Blackwell informed against Masterson, and to " obtain his own freedom brought others into bonds."

He "so won the bishop's favors (but lost the Lord's) as Bradford tells us, as he was not only dismissed, but in open court the archbishop gave him great applause and his solemn blessing to proceed in his voyage."

The report of these disheartening circumstances was communicated to the church at Plymouth, and in view of them, " a day of humiliation was appointed to seek the Lord for his direction."

" The pastor took the text, 1 Sam. xxiii. 3, 4: ' And David's men said unto him, see, we be afraid here in Judah, how much more if we come to Keilah against the host of the Philistines? Then David asked counsel of the Lord again,' etc. From which text he taught many things very aptly, and befitting their present occasion and condition, strengthening them against their fears and perplexities, and encouraging them in their resolutions. After which they concluded both what number and what persons should prepare themselves to go with the first; for all that were willing to have gone could not get ready for their other affairs in so short a time;

neither if all could have been ready, had there been means to have transported them altogether. Those that stayed, being the greater number, required the pastor to stay with them; and indeed for other reasons he could not then well go, and so it was the more easily yielded unto. The other then desired the elder, Mr. Brewster, to go with them, which was also consented unto. It was also agreed on, by mutual consent and covenant, that those that went should be an absolute church of themselves, as well as those that stayed; seeing in such a dangerous voyage, and a removal to such a distance, it might come to pass they should (for the body of them) never meet again in this world; yet with this proviso, that as any of the rest came over to them, or of the other returned upon occasion, they should be reputed as members, without any further dismission or testimonial. It was also promised to those that were first, by the body of the rest, that if the Lord gave them life, and means, and opportunity, they would come to them as soon as they could."

XVIII.

BREWER AND BREWSTER, THE BROWNIST PRINTERS.

THE interruption in the course of the anxious negotiations for the means of departure to America, caused by the proceedings of the English authorities in reference to Brewster and his partner in the printing establishment, claims special and more extended notice than it has hitherto received. If we suspend the narrative to enter circumstantially into this peculiar case, it must be remembered that there was a practical diversion in it from the object sought by the Pilgrims.

Thomas Brewer, who supplied to Brewster the capital for the printing-office, was a man of high respectability, and a member of the university at Leyden. There was no reason to warrant the charge, brought either against Brewster or his patron, of violating the law. At the instance of the English authorities, a regulation had been made to prevent the further printing of English books in favor of non-conformity. On the promulgation of that order,

Brewster ceased to print works of the kind prohibited. Sir Dudley Carleton, the ambassador, demanded that he should be arrested nevertheless, in order to an investigation. His own search for him was most persevering. On the 19th of July, 1619, Matthew Slade writes from Amsterdam to Sir Dudley:* "I have made the best inquiry that I could concerning William Brewster amongst them that know him well; but cannot hear otherwise than that he is yet dwelling and resident at Leyden. Neither is it likely that he will remove his dwelling hither, there being another English printer, named William Thorp, also a Brownist, settled here. If he lurk here, for fear of apprehension, it will be hard to find him."

Three days after this communication (July 22, 1619), in writing to Secretary Naunton, from the Hague, the ambassador says: "One William Brewster, a Brownist, hath been for some years an inhabitant and printer at Leyden, but is now within three weeks removed from thence, and gone back to dwell in London, where he may be found out and examined." "Aug. 20. I have made good inquiry after William Brewster, at Leyden, and am well assured that he is not returned thither; neither is it likely he will, having removed from thence his family and goods." "Sep. 12. In my last I advertised your honor that Brewster was taken at Leyden;

* State Paper, MSS.

which proved an error, in that the scout, who was employed by the magistrates for his apprehension, being a dull, drunken fellow, took one man for another. But Brewer, who set him on work, and being a man of means, bare the charge of his printing, is fast in the University's prison; and his printing letters, which were found in his house in a garret, where he had hid them, and his books and papers, are all sealed up. I expect to-morrow to receive his voluntary confession of such books as he hath caused to be printed by Brewster, for this year and a half or two years past."

No time was lost in pressing the case as against Brewer. The university having exclusive jurisdiction, civil and criminal, over its members, took cognizance of the complaint of the ambassador against the printer. An English agent was sent by Sir Dudley Carleton to watch the proceedings. On the 18th September, 1619, he writes to Secretary Naunton: "I advertised your honor of Brewer's being laid fast in the university's prison at Leyden. I have sent an advocate of this town, who understands our language, and a servant of mine, expressly to visit his books and papers, and to present certain interrogatories to those who examine him. Whereof I send your honor the translates with his answers, which are so indirect that they give no man satisfaction that sees them, and therefore I have now used the Prince of Orange's authority, who hath spoken to the rector of the university, not to give the prisoner liberty until His Majesty's pleasure be known concerning him, which the rector doth promise shall be fulfilled, notwithstanding that the whole company of Brownists doth offer caution for Brewer, and he being a university man, the scholars are likewise stirred up by the Brownists to plead privilege in that kind."

The Schepens and council wrote September 19, 1619, "to Jacob Von Brouchhoven, deputy councillor of their High Mightinesses," in the following terms:

"We have to-day summoned into our presence Thomas Brewer, an Englishman, and he being heard, we learn that his business heretofore has been printing, or having printing done, but in consequence of the publication of the *placaat* in relation to the printing of books, he had stopped the printing-office, which was at that time mostly his own; and that his partner was a certain William Brewster, who was also in town at present, but sick. We have therefore resolved, after having communicated with the Rector Magnificus (the head of the university) to deliver the said Thomas* Brewer, who is a member of the university, in the place where it is the

* The name is given variously in the records William and Thomas, but properly it was Thomas Brewer.

custom to bring the members thereof; and in regard to William Brewster, to bring him, inasmuch as he is sick, into the debtor's chamber, provisionally, where he went voluntarily. Of which things we have thought proper to inform you, and to await further orders in the matter."

The "Schepens and council," though not "drunken," seem to have been as "dull" as the "schout." They were equally mistaken, with the officer, as to the apprehension of Brewster.

They apologized to Brouchhoven on the 23d of September. "We have," they write, "this day, in consequence of your letter, summoned the officer, and strongly enjoined upon him to do his best to arrest William Brewster, in whose person he was mistaken, which he has promised to do, but at the same time said he had heard that the said William Brewster had already left. A meeting was held to-day at the rector's, in regard to the case of Thomas Brewer."

The prisoner now being in the charge of the university, they proceeded to impound his effects; the following is from the "criminal and civil record:"

"Upon the application of Loth Huyghensz Gael, bailiff of the university, to have an assessor and schepenmaster, to assist him in seizing the types of Thomas Brewer, a member of said university, now in prison, and in searching his library for any works printed or caused to be printed by him within a year and a half or thereabouts, and in seizing the same, and in examining him as to what books he has printed or caused to be printed within a year and a half, either in English or in other languages, the rector and judges of the said university have appointed, and by these presents do appoint, Dr. Johannes Polyander, assessor, and Dr. Gulielmus Bontius, schepenmaster, provisionally only, for the seizure of the type and searching of the library aforesaid, and seizing the books.

"In pursuance whereof the types found in the garret are seized, the great door nailed in two places, and the seal of the said officer, impressed in green wax over paper, is placed upon the lock and nails; a catalogue is made of the books; and the chamber, where the same were found, is sealed with the aforesaid seal upon the lock and nails. Done the 21st September, 1619. In my presence, J. Vervey."

Two days after, the warrant was issued to examine Brewer:

"On this 23d September, 1619, the honorable rector and judges of the university in the city of Leyden have, upon the application of Loth Huyghensz Gael, bailiff of the university, appointed, and by these presents do appoint, Dr. Cornelis Swaneburg assessor, and Dr. Gulielmus Bontius schepenmaster, to examine Thomas Brewer, in custody of the said bailiff, as to what books he has within a year and a half past printed, or caused to be printed, in the Latin, English, or other languages; and the said assessor and Jan Bout Jacobsz, schepenmaster, shall cause the type of the said Brewer which have been seized, to be brought, for better keeping, from his house to the University rooms. Which is accordingly done the day and year aforesaid in my presence, Jacob J. Vervey."

The great offence which the English ambassador was anxious to prove against the Pilgrim printer was, that of allowing his press to be used by the Presbyterians of Scotland, when they were denied an opportunity to print works, in defence of their views, in their own country. Two books in particular Sir Dudley mentions: *De Regimine Ecclesiæ Scotianæ* and the *Perth Assembly*, " of which," says the offended ambassador, " if he was not the printer himself, he assuredly knows both the printer and the author." Because of this suspicion, he was determined, if possible, to get Brewster within his grasp. He was completely foiled, and, disappointed in his prey, he resolved to torment Brewer.

Sir Dudley Carleton writes to Secretary Naunton, Nov. 3, 1619:

" RIGHT HONORABLE, — One of the curators and rector of the University of Leyden, with Polyander and Heinsius, came to me on Monday last, being the first of this present, expressly from Leyden, to let me know their resolution to send Brewer into England; which, for preservation of the privileges of their university, they made appeal unto me, by a writing unto Brewer's hand, to proceed of his own desire, as a dutiful subject to His Majesty, and willing to give His Majesty all satisfaction. But first, he required of them in the said writing to be assured it is His Majesty's own pleasure to have him sent; next, that he may go as a free man, under caution of his lands and goods, not as a prisoner; then, that he may not be punished, during his abode in England, either in body or goods; and that he may be suffered to return hither in a competent time; and lastly, that his journey be without his own charge.

"These things were requested of me by the curator, the rector, and the rest in his behalf; wherein I made them this verbal promise, without being further moved by any of them (as I was formerly) to give them any act in writing; that for the first, it was His Majesty's will and pleasure, which I might better assure them, having the same now a second time reiterated unto me by your honor's letters of the 23d of October, which at that instant I received. Next, that if they would take caution of him of his lands and goods for his rendering himself to His Majesty in England, I left it to their discretions; but to send him as a free man could not well be, as long as he remained in *reatu*.

"Then, that for his body and goods, during his abode in England, I undertook he should not be touched (being so warranted by your honor's former letters of the 21st of September), and for his return, that it should be within the space of three months at the furthest, and sooner, if he dealt ingenuously and freely in his confession.

"Touching the charge of his journey, I made no difficulty to free both him and them thereof, not doubting but His Majesty will be pleased to allow it; so as there remaining this only point of difference between us, whether he should go as a prisoner, or as a free man; in the end we concluded of a middle way betwixt both, that he should go *sub libera custodia*, being attended from Leyden to Rotterdam by one of the beadles, with another officer of the University, and be there delivered to some such person as I should appoint for his safe convoy into England, where I have undertaken for him, he shall not be cast into any common prison, nor be ill used; though, for his liberty, I let them know he must not expect it, but according as he shall merit it by the satisfaction he shall give His Majesty; wherein if he fail of what he now seems willing to perform, the fear of being returned back hither again to the place where he hath lain ever since his first apprehension, and where he may be long enough, unless he be delivered by His Majesty's grace and favor, will be a sufficient torture. But, on the other side, if he carry himself well and dutifully, I will beseech your honor to be a means to His Majesty, that he may be well treated, and sent back with contentment; the rather, because he hath taken his resolution of presenting himself unto His Majesty against the minds of some stiffnecked men in Leyden, who endeavored to dissuade him. And it will give all inferior persons encouragement by his example, according to the like occasions, willingly to submit themselves; he being a gentleman of a good house, both of land and living; which none of his profession in these parts are; though through the reveries of his religion (he being, as I advertised your honor, a professed Brownist) he hath mortgaged and consumed a great part of his estate."

Carleton writes November 28, 1619: " The States' fleet now prepared against the pirates could not possibly put to sea until this day; which is the first easterly wind we have had for these six weeks past.

" I hope it will carry over Sir William Zouch with Mr. Brewer to your honor, who have lain long together at Flushing; and his fellow Brownists at Leyden are somewhat scandalized, because they hear Sir William hath taught him to drink health."

Sir Dudley Carleton writes to Secretary Naunton, January 29, 1619–20: "I have acquainted the curators of the University of Leyden with the good treatment which hath been given unto Brewer, far beyond his deserving, and with his delivery; for which they render His Majesty humble thanks, and at his return hither, unless he undertake to them to do his uttermost in finding out Brewster (wherein I will not fail likewise of all other endeavors), he is not like to be at liberty; the suspicion whereof, I believe, keeps him from hence, for as yet he appears not in these parts."

The university authorities calmly asserted their rights, and would not surrender Brewer to the imperious demand of Sir Dudley, without some guarantee for his return to Holland in safety. Their virtual protest against his violence is recorded in the register of the university.

"At an extraordinary meeting of the curators and burgomasters held on the 21st of October, 1619, —

"It being represented to the curators and burgomasters that the ambassador of His Royal Majesty, the king of Great Britain, requested that Thomas Brewer, English gentleman, who is now confined in the prison of the university upon the complaint of the said ambassador, by order of the rector and assessors, might be taken from here to His Royal Majesty in England, it is resolved, after consulting with the rector and assessors, that the said Brewer shall still be offered, as before, to the said ambassador for further examination in the presence of any one whom His Excellency may be pleased to appoint, or he shall go before His Excellency himself, or, otherwise, a proper obligation shall be demanded from His Excellency, to the effect that the said Brewer shall be restored here again within two months, which he not consenting to, the matter must be referred to the high and mighty lords the States of Holland and West Friesland."

With a certain nobleness strongly contrasted with the spy-like manœuvres of his persecutors, Brewer offered to go to the king of England, and to meet any inquiry, so that he were not ensnared, on a mere pretence, into the power of the bishops.

Apparently for his own protection, the magistrates of Leyden required of Brewer, that he should enter into a bond to return to the country.

" Before the undersigned, assessor of the University and schepenmaster in the city of Leyden, appeared Thomas Brewer, English gentleman, a member of the said university, at present detained in custody by the bailiff of the same, and declared that whereas he has determined, upon the urgent desire of His Royal Majesty of Great Britain, to betake himself voluntarily unto His Majesty, and is permitted to make the journey in honorable company: therefore he has bound himself, and hereby does bind himself, to go upon the said journey, and here again to return in the company which shall be provided for him, as well on behalf of the honorable rector and judges of the said university, as of the ambassador of His Majesty; and to be faithful hereto, without going off or leaving, directly or indirectly, in any manner, under penalty of his person and property, movable and unmovable, present or future, and rights of action and claims, nothing excepted, and wheresoever the same may be, being subject to the execution of all laws and judges. All in good faith and without fraud. Done the 12th of November, 1619.

"(sd.) Swanenburg. D. VAN ALPHEN."

These preliminaries being settled, Brewer, in the company of his friends, departed from Leyden on the same day, to commit himself to the "honorable" charge of Sir W. Zouche. Writing from Rotterdam, November 13, 1619, to Sir Dudley Carleton, Sir William says: "I was last night almost out of hope of having my expected company, but about ten of the clock, Mr. Brewer arrived, conveyed hitherto by the beadle of the University, Mr. Robinson and Mr. Kebel, accompanied by two other of his friends. Their names I think are not worth the asking. We go forward about two or three of the clock. If we find not a boat, we intend to be at Dort this night.

The gentleman seems very ready and willing to go with me, and hath good hope of his despatch and happy issue, if he be not referred to the judgment of the bishops, concerning which he says he made caution before his departure, and if you have not written so much already, he desires you will do so when you write next to Mr. Secretary. He excuses his long stay by reason of the sudden warning he had to provide him. He demanded of me if I had order to defray him. I have told him, yes. He is contented, but says it was not his desire, nor mentioned by him. I assure your Lordship I will make no delay, but take the speediest opportunities to be rid of this employment."

A brief original note in French dated " *De Leyde*, 16 *de Nov.*, 1619, *au Myn Heer Carleton*," shows that Polyander was in communication with the English ambassador on the subject.

Rough weather detained Brewer some time longer in Holland, and, during this interval, his friends made strenuous efforts to obtain his freedom. In a second letter to Sir Dudley from Flushing (26 of November, 1619), Sir William Zouche says:

" I have waited a wind these ten days, but can get none good, nor fair weather. No day hath passed without a storm, and some of them so rude, as the streets in some places have run with salt-water that hath scaled the walls, and in other it hath made pools and lakes, and kept the people within their own doors. A ship, with a mast lost, brought news of a tilt-boat drowned, wherein were above thirty of them, — about seven saved. George Martin is this day arrived, having been nine days between Rotterdam and here. , I have had scarce any opportunity to go over into Flanders, and Mr. Brewer is very unwilling to go that way in this bad weather. He hath many friends in Middleboro, and those exceeding earnest in his cause, as the treasurer-general, his brother, the chief of the reckon chamber, and his other brother, a minister (their name is Teebake), and one Mr. Vosberg, chief reckon master, who was on the way toward Holland to speak to His Excellency on Mr. Brewer's behalf, and to have advised him to have challenged the privileges of the university and of the town, by which he should have had his trial there. They told me many stories of it, and how an earl of Holland had been denied to have a prisoner out of the town. I was on Monday, was sevennight, invited to dinner by them, wherein they did expostulate in the business; as how great a power our king hath here as to have a prisoner (after he had been kept in prison longer than the law of the land doth allow) to be sent to him almost with breach of their privileges, and that he shall ever have the same power, if he perform the conditions made by your Lordship, his ambassador (who will not abuse them, but have authority from His Majesty for all goods). But if the conditions are broken, they will be more wary to satisfy his demand again in the same kind, or to trust your Lordship; and if there be any occasion, they will write and send in his behalf, and have persuaded me to signify so much to His Majesty. I have promised to tell so much to Mr. Secretary and to the king, if it please him to question with me concerning him. Otherwise I durst not of myself, speak with him about it. I was much importuned as if I had been a great man, and have had many promises of their loves and friendship, if I can show him any, and they being my lords and paymasters may do it if it please them."

What reception Brewer met with in England is unknown to us. Sir Dudley, in a letter dated Jan. 19, 1620, says: "Unless Brewer undertakes to do his uttermost in finding out Brewster (wherein I will not fail likewise of all other endeavors), he is not like to be at liberty; the suspicion whereof keeps him from hence, for as yet he appears not in these parts."

The following entry in the Leyden records shows that the press was watched with sleepless care.

"At a meeting held the 9th of May, 1620." "A certain memorial of the Ambassador Carleton is read to the effect that the types and papers of Brewer might remain in keeping here. It is resolved to keep the said types as hitherto."

We might almost imagine that the whole movement of the ambassador and his party was intended to prevent the Pilgrims from taking the printing materials to America. Brewer returned to Leyden. It is stated that, in 1627, he sold out his property and effects in Leyden, and returned to England. In a memorandum, in the state paper office, London, dated September 16, 1626, we read that Thomas Brewer coming not long since from Amsterdam, where he became a perfect Brownist, and being a man of good estate, is the general patron of the Kentish Brownists; who (by his means) daily and dangerously increase, the said Brewer hath provided a most pestilent book beyond the seas. " One Turner of Sutton Valance in Kent, seems to be a chaplain of his, and preaches in houses, barns, and woods."

" He hath many followers and is maintained principally by the said Thomas Brewer." He was not suffered to remain long unmolested after his return from Holland. Archbishop Laud cast him into prison where he remained nearly fourteen years, and was liberated by an order from the House of Commons, November 28, 1640. What if Brewster had been seized instead of Brewer? Would he have commanded the same influence in Holland?

Not being a member of the university, would he

have had the same support against the demands of the ambassador? Once in the power of the bishops in England, would he have experienced the same fate as that of Brewer at a later period? If so, what would have been the effect on the Pilgrim enterprise? On a thread so slender were suspended the destinies of the people who laid the foundation of American greatness. Who can fail to recognize the hand of God in directing their course, amidst all their weakness and peril?

XIX.

CUSHMAN'S NEGOTIATIONS. — THE MAYFLOWER.

BREWSTER is safe in London, but Cushman writes, he is "not well at this time; whether he will come back to you or go into the north, I yet know not." Brewster scarcely knows himself in what direction to return from his pursuers. Carver, in attending to matters at Southampton, was absent frequently from London.

The conduct of affairs with the Virginia company and the merchant adventurers, devolved mainly on Cushman. "In all businesses," Bradford says, "the acting part is most difficult." The more energetic messenger of the Leyden church had to do the work in London, and, as a natural consequence, to bear the blame.

The first point was to obtain a patent from the Virginia company. Unhappily, the company was so agitated by internal dissensions, that it was extremely difficult to obtain a hearing for any business whatever. Sir Edwin Sandys, the patron of the Pilgrims, became obnoxious to the king. Under these circumstances, it is a wonder that the application, in reference to their proposal to emigrate, was received with the slightest favor. Success in the negotiation would be altogether unaccountable, if we did not know the financial exigencies of the company. Vast sums of money had been expended previously in attempts "to make a plantation," without a single satisfactory result. The power, wisdom, and enterprise of the first men of their age, had proved ineffectual for the accomplishment of an object, nevertheless intensely desired. The Virginia company had all the means and appliances for colonization, — except suitable men willing to go out and form a settlement. Men they wanted who would take root in the country, finding a home in any clime, from the stability of their habits, the warmth of their affections, and the simplicity of their object; — men of sound mind, clear conscience, firm purpose, all-enduring patience, of practical skill and persevering diligence; — men who would give themselves to the work of colonization for the advantage of posterity, and who had no thought or desire to return laden with the material wealth that would add to their personal consequence or social distinction at home; — men who had crucified the love of ease, and in whom was quenched the lust of fame; — men willing to be forgotten or unknown, so that they might lay in silence and obscurity the foundations of a superstructure that should remain to the end of time. Such men had been called into existence for a quarter of a century or more, and were willing to expatriate themselves under any conditions that were practicable and compatible with their sense of moral rectitude.

But from the veil of prejudice that obscured their vision, they could not recognize them in their true character. It never occurred to promoters of colonization that people who would lose reputation, and suffer the loss of home, of personal freedom, to linger in loathsome dungeons, or die on the gibbet, rather than violate conscience in relation to the worship of God, must have the stamina of principle required for this peculiar service.

They spurned the petition sent to them in 1592 from those who were "falsely called Brownists," and, in the mean time, tried every class of adventures that might be lured to the new world by illusive expectation of finding "Paradise regained," or exhaustless mines of gold. The ridiculous failure at Sagadahoc of the famous expedition promoted by Lord Chief Justice Popham, the judge who condemned Penry to die, the disasters at Jamestown, and the more recent ill-fated voyages which caused so much odium in London, destroyed confidence in all such schemes. They began to fear that the most wretched class of persons would prefer to stay in England, than to venture to wild and desolate regions in which so many had perished, or who had sent tidings to their friends so melancholy and disheartening.

Even Sir Edwin Sandys proposed to enforce the transportation of a hundred miserable children in the streets of London, who were unwilling to go, in the hope that they might make pioneers in Virginia. "Under severe masters," he says, "they might be brought to goodness."

We must not blame too severely these Elizabethan sages for their want of discernment, and their slowness of apprehension under the instruction of the royal "Solomon" who succeeded the virgin queen. After the experience of three centuries, the statesmen of England have yet to learn fully, that conscientiousness in matters of religion is no just cause for political or social disability. There are still not a few who speak of nonconformity as "rebellion" against the church established by act of parliament.

If the council of Virginia could have acted with transparent honesty, and if their sentiments might have been spoken frankly, and in unison with the facts of the case, there would have been no necessity for the Pilgrim negotiators to represent their views with so much secrecy and caution, and through second parties. The president of the council might have said: "Let John Carver, Robert Cushman, and William Brewster come into the council room. (They need not kneel.) Representatives of the English exiles in Leyden. Speaking for ourselves and for the English court, we greet you well.

"It goeth hard with us that we should ever have to make use of a "Brownist," in trying to make a plantation. But we are shut up to this course. We hung some of your fathers, and we starved others in the prisons of this city. We banished many of your company to Newfoundland, and we have tried to make your exile in Holland as uncomfortable as we had the power to do. Our aim has been to destroy you, but we have failed in this object, and we hear that your numbers are rather increasing. Our efforts have been also directed to plant colonies in the world which lieth to the west. We advised with Lord Bacon and Sir Walter Raleigh. We sent out our best commanders, and furnished the ships with stores of provisions. That the planters might not be discouraged, we ordered the vessels to return with fresh supplies, but the new settlers took the first opportunity to come back. In these two things we have been disappointed; we have not utterly suppressed your conventicles, and we have not made a settlement in America. You shall go there, since you wish it.

The lord bishops have tried to make you hypocrites that you may do less harm. But if you will not say that you believe things contrary to your real convictions, in this emergency the court of King James and the Virginia company will excuse you."

No speech of this kind has been found in the national archives. What may exist " in cipher " we cannot tell. Sir Ferdinando Gorges, however, who is a most competent witness, gives us a fair idea of the argument which ultimately prevailed with the Virginia company.

With admirable naïveté Sir Ferdinando tells us: the Virginia company "were forced, through the great charge they had been at, to hearken to any propositions that might give ease and furtherance to so hopeful business. To that purpose it was referred to their considerations how necessary it was, that means might be used to draw into those enterprises some of those families that had retired themselves into Holland for scruple of conscience, giving them such freedom and liberty as might stand with their likings. This advice being hearkened unto, there were that undertook the putting it in practice."

A patent was at length obtained under the seal of the Virginia company, " not taken in the name of their own company, but in the name of Mr. John Wincob, a religious gentleman then belonging to the Countess of Lincoln, who intended to go with them." As the lands conveyed by it were not occupied, it never acquired practical value. They had in this, as in all other things, to rest on God's providence.

The opposition of the "powers and principalities" being so far neutralized, Cushman sought to effect the best arrangement with the merchant adventurers for raising the needful capital. The position of Cushman was trying. He stood alone, and had to reconcile conflicting interests. He showed the articles of the Pilgrims (left in his care by Carver) to Mr. Weston one of the principal adventurers, but he strongly disapproved of their proposition to acquire separate property in the first instance, and to be masters of a certain portion of their time. On hearing of this clause, Sir George Farrer and his brother withdrew 500*l*. from the undertaking. To have pressed the condition would have been to alienate the rest of the adventurers. Rather than abandon the design at the last moment, Cushman consented to the only terms on which the necessary coöperation of the adventurers could be obtained. They wanted security for the advancement of their capital, and since the Pilgrims had no property to offer for that purpose, Cushman agreed to mortgage their labor for seven years, and to allow their stock with improvements, to remain for that term, prior to its distribution according to the amount of shares.

The brethren at Leyden were dissatisfied, and their disappointment was the greater from the offer of better terms made to them by the Dutch. In a joint letter, dated June 10, 1620, Samuel Fuller, William Bradford, Isaac Allerton, and Edward Winslow, addressed a serious remonstrance to Carver and Cushman, requiring them not to exceed the bounds of their commission.

Four days after, Robinson wrote to Carver, expressing his regret and disappointment in the terms agreed upon by Cushman. "Mr. Weston," he says, "makes himself merry with our endeavors about buying a ship, but we have done nothing in this but with good reason, as I am persuaded, nor yet that I know in any thing else, save in these two: the one, that we employed Robert Cushman, who is known (though a good man, and of special abilities in his kind, yet) most unfit to deal for other men, by reason of his singularity and too great indifferency for any conditions, and for (to speak truly) we have had nothing from him but terms and presumptions.

"The other, that we have so much relied, by implicit faith, as it were, upon generalities, without seeing the particular course and means for so weighty an affair set down unto us."

After all, it is fairly questionable, whether any of the Pilgrim brethren would have acted with equal vigor and discretion. At a subsequent stage in the proceedings, the entire company offered what they considered to be an amendment on Cushman's agreement, which, if acted upon, would have involved them in far greater trouble and difficulty. They lived to do justice to his integrity and decision, and spoke of him as their "right hand man" in these transactions. His case affords an instructive example of the advantage secured by thorough honesty of purpose, in perplexing and critical affairs, when the highest worldly sagacity alone would fail.

Cushman replied to the "paper of reasons framed against the clause in the conditions" in two letters. The first of these communications Carver judiciously kept back to avoid giving offence. The writer felt deeply, and expressed his mind freely. He was almost worn out with the trials and distractions he had borne alone in London for many months.

"Neither my mind nor my body," he says, "is at liberty to do much, for I am fettered with business, and had rather study to be quiet, than to make answer to their exceptions." His first thought, on receiving the complaining letters, was to relinquish the business altogether. "The many discouragements I find here," he writes, "together with the demurs and retirings there, made me to say, I would give up my accounts to John Carver, and at his coming acquaint him fully with all my courses, and so leave it quite, with only the poor clothes on my back. But, gathering up myself by further consideration, I resolved to make one trial more, and to acquaint Mr. Weston with the fainted state of our business; and though he hath been much discontented at some things amongst us of late, which hath made him often say that, save for his purpose, he would not meddle at all with the business any more, yet, considering how far we were plunged into matters, and how it stood both on our credits and undoing, at the last he gathered up himself a little more, and coming to me two hours after, he told me he would not leave it. And so advising together we resolved to hire a ship, and have took liking of one (the *Mayflower*) till Monday, about 60 last,* for a greater we cannot get, except it be too great; but a fine ship it is."

How much depends upon a man "gathering himself up" in time. Cushman had relieved his mind by writing the letter to the Pilgrims, though they did not receive it. He had answered their objections in his own style, and felt he could breathe more freely. For example, amongst other things they had said: "This will hinder the building of good and fair houses, contrary to the advice of politics." Cushman replied: "So we would have it; our purpose is to build for the present such houses as, if need be, we may with little grief set

---

* About 120 tons.

a fire, and run away by the light; our riches shall not be in pomp, but in strength; if God send us riches, we will employ them to provide more men, ships, munition, etc. You may see it among the best politics, that a commonwealth is readier to ebb than to flow, when once fine houses and gay clothes come up."

Refreshed by these utterances, Cushman set about completing the bargain for the Mayflower, and hired Mr. Clark as pilot, who had been to Virginia the year before.

Carver wrote to Cushman to complain of his negligence, but the summer was passing away, and Cushman felt no time should be lost in recrimination. In reply from London, June 10, 1620, he said: "All that I have power to do here, shall not be one hour behind, I warrant you." "I have received from Leyden, since you went, three or four letters directed to you, though they only concern me. I will not trouble you with them.

"We have reckoned, it should seem, without our host; and, counting upon 150 persons, there cannot be found above 1200*l.* and odd moneys of all the ventures you can reckon, besides some cloth, stockings, and shoes, which are not counted; so we shall come short 300*l.* or 400*l.*" He tells Carver that he will obtain more money, and concludes: "For Mr.

Crab (the minister), of whom you write, he hath promised to go with us, yet I tell you I shall not be without fear till I see him shipped, for he is much opposed, yet I hope he will not fail. Think the best of all, and bear with patience what is wanting, and the Lord guide us all."

XX.

THE DEBARKATION FROM LEYDEN.

THE *Mayflower* sailed from the Thames. No vessel ever left the port of London, the name of which is associated with such undying interest. Yet we are left to conjecture the circumstances of her departure. Was Sabin Staresmore (the active and faithful member of the church in Southwark, who had rendered such untiring service for the messengers from Leyden), liberated from prison? Did Henry Jacob, with the members of his flock, come to bid farewell to the Pilgrims from London? Were Mr. Sherley, Mr. Hatherly, Mr. Andrews, and Mr. Hatherly the friendly adventurers, who were merchants in the city, present? "No man knoweth." It was the purpose of Him who "bringeth to nought things that are, by things that are not," to suffer the ship, since so renowned, to leave her moorings without notice or record, and to glide down the river as the most ordinary craft that ever sailed. Yet, if the brethren met for prayer in London with their companions in the faith and patience of Jesus, when they began to negotiate with the Virginia company, we must believe that their hearts were uplifted, though it might be in silence, for a blessing on the enterprise, and that they wept in sympathy and affection for those who ventured themselves in the memorable voyage. The "men of Kent" were deeply interested in the undertaking, and surely at Greenwich the friends of Cushman would come to cheer him on, and join in saying with him, "a fine ship she is."

At Leyden the Pilgrims had liberty to meet for prayer without the danger of imprisonment, or of being pelted by an ignorant and bigoted mob.

Any stranger who passed through the street in which stands the ancient church of St. Peters, on the 20th of July, 1620, must have stayed awhile to listen to the strains of vocal melody, sounding sweetly from the large house of the pastor near the belfry. It is toward evening. The day has been spent in the religious exercises which, according to the custom of the Pilgrims, preceded every new undertaking.

In the morning Robinson spoke to them at considerable length from Ezra viii. 21. " And there, at the river Chava, I proclaimed a fast, that we might humble ourselves before our God, and seek of Him a right way for us and for our children, and for all our substance."

"Amongst other wholesome instructions and exhortations," Winslow tells us, he said:

"We are now erelong to part asunder, and the Lord knoweth whether ever he should live to see our faces again. But whether the Lord had appointed it or not, he charged us, before God and his blessed angels, to follow him no further than he followed Christ; and if God should reveal any thing to us by any other instrument of his, to be ready to receive it as ever we were to receive any truth by his ministry; for he was very confident the Lord had more truth and light to break forth out of His holy word. He took occasion, also, miserably to bewail the state and condition of the reformed churches, who were come to a period in religion, and would go no further than the instruments of their reformation.

"As, for example, the Lutherans, they could not be drawn to go beyond what Luther saw; for whatever part of God's will he had further imparted and revealed to Calvin, they will rather die than embrace it. And so also, saith he, you see the Calvinists, they stick where he left them; a misery much to be lamented; for though they were precious shining lights in their times, yet God had not revealed his whole will to them; and were they now living, saith he, they would be as ready and willing to embrace further light as that they had received. Here also he put us in mind of our church covenant, at least that part of it whereby we promise and covenant with God and one with another, to receive whatsoever light or truth shall be made known to us from His written word; but withal exhorted us to take heed what we received for truth, and well to examine and compare it and weigh it with other Scriptures of truth before we received it. For, saith he, it is not possible the Christian world should come so lately out of such thick antichristian darkness, and that full perfection of knowledge should break forth at once.

"Another thing he commended to us, was that we should use all means to avoid and shake off the name of Brownist, being a mere nickname and brand to make religion odious, and the professors of it to the Christian world. And to that end, said he, I should be glad if some godly minister would go over with you before my coming; there will be no difference between the unconformable ministers (the Puritans) and you, when they come to the practice of the ordinances out of the kingdom; and so advised us by all means to close with the godly party of the kingdom of England, and rather to study union than diversion, namely, how near we might possibly without sin close with them, than in the least measure to affect division or separation from them. And be not loath to take another pastor or teacher, saith he; for that flock that hath two shepherds is not endangered, but secured by it."

One portion of the counsel of Robinson has received more attention than another part of it, with which, however, it stands essentially connected.

Our progress may be at "express" rate, but it will be seen, on a careful examination of the words of Robinson, that he does not recommend us to go "off the line."

The thoughts of the morrow, and of its sad partings, would arise in the midst of the pastor's sage discourse, and tears flowed abundantly.

But, says Winslow, "we refreshed ourselves, after tears, with singing of psalms, making joyful melody in our hearts, as well as with the voice, there being many of our congregation very expert in music; and indeed it was the sweetest melody than ever mine ears heard."

On the following day (July 21, 1620), the emigrant party, "accompanied with most of their brethren out of the city," took their journey to Delfthaven on the Meuse, a distance of fourteen miles, where the *Speedwell* (a vessel of 60 tuns) was ready to receive them.

"So they left that goodly and pleasant city, which had been their resting-place near twelve years; but they knew they were *Pilgrims*, and looked not much on those things, but lift up their eyes to the heavens, their dearest country, and quieted their spirits.

"When they came to the place, they found the ship and all things ready; and such of their friends as could not come with them followed after them, and sundry also came from Amsterdam (thirty-six miles distant) to see them shipped, and to take leave of them. That night was spent with little sleep by the most, but with friendly entertainment and Christian love. The next day (July 22, 1620), the wind being fair, they went aboard, and their friends with them, where truly doleful was the sight of that sad and mournful parting; to see what sights and sobs and prayers did sound amongst them, what tears did gush from every eye, and pithy speeches pierced each heart; that sundry of the Dutch strangers, that stood on the quay as spectators, could not refrain from tears. Yet comfortable and sweet it was to see such lively expressions of dear and unfeigned love. But the tide (which stays for no man) calling them away that were thus loathe to depart, their reverend pastor falling down on his knees (and they all with him), with watery cheeks commended them with most fervent prayers to the Lord and his blessing. And thus with mutual embraces and many tears, they took their leaves one of another, which proved to be the last leave to many of them."

Finally the ship was cleared, and the sails hoisted. A volley of small shot and three pieces of ordnance were fired, and the Pilgrims left the harbor. With a prosperous wind they came in a short time to Southampton, where they found the Mayflower " come from London, lying ready, with all the rest of their company." " After a joyful welcome and mutual congratulations, with other friendly entertainments, they fell to parley about their business, how to despatch with the best expedition; as also with their agents, about the alteration of their conditions. Mr. Carver pleaded he was employed here at Southampton, and knew not well what the other had done at London. Mr. Cushman answered, he had done nothing but what he was urged to, partly by the grounds of equity, and more especially by necessity; otherwise all had been dashed and many undone."

Mr. Weston came from London to see them despatched, and to have the conditions confirmed. The Pilgrims declined, on the ground that they were not according to the original agreement, neither could they yield to them without the consent of the rest that were behind. Mr. Weston was "much offended, and told them they must look to stand on their own legs. So he returned in displeasure."

" And whereas they wanted well near 100*l*. to clear things at their going away, he would not take order to disburse a penny, but left them shift as they could. So they were forced to sell some of their provisions to stop this gap, which was some three or four score firkins of butter, which commodity they might best spare, having provided too large a quantity of that kind."

To counteract the influence of the angry Mr. Weston, the Pilgrims wrote a letter August 3, 1620, to the merchant adventurers in London, explaining the case, closing in this strain: " We are in such a strait at present, as we are forced to sell away 60*l*. worth of our provisions to clear the haven, and withal put ourselves upon great extremities, scarce having any butter, no oil, not a shoe to mend a shoe, nor every man a sword to his side, wanting many muskets, much armor, etc. And yet we are willing to expose ourselves to such imminent dangers as are like to ensue, and trust to the good providence of God, rather than his name and truth should be evil spoken of for us. Thus saluting all of you in love, and beseeching the Lord to give a blessing to our endeavor, and keep all our hearts in the bonds of peace, we take leave and rest."

The loss of the butter and the want of muskets, perhaps, on the whole, was better for them.

Five days after the sailing of the *Speedwell* from

Delft Haven (July 27, 1620), Robinson, in his thoughtful kindness, wrote a letter to Carver enclosing " a large letter to the whole," admirably adapted to tranquillize and sustain their minds amidst these perplexities and troubles.

To Carver, Robinson says : " My dear brother, — I have a true feeling of your perplexity of mind and toil of body, but I hope that you, who have always been able so plentifully to administer comfort unto others in these trials, are so well furnished for yourself, as that far greater difficulties than you have yet undergone (though I conceive them to have been great enough), cannot oppress you, though they press you, as the apostle speaketh. ' The spirit of a man (sustained by the Spirit of God) will sustain his infirmities,' Prov. xviii. 14. I doubt not, so will yours. . . . . My heart is with you. . . . The Lord in whom you trust, and whom you serve, ever in this business and journey, guide you with His hand, protect you with His love, and show us His salvation in the end, and bring us in the mean while together in the place desired (if such be His good will), for His Christ's sake, amen."

The letter of Robinson to the Pilgrim emigrants is full of tenderness and wisdom. " Loving Christian friends," he says, " I do humbly and in the Lord salute you, as being those with whom I am present in my best affections, and most earnest longings after you, though I be constrained for a while to be bodily absent from you. I say constrained, God knowing how willingly, and much rather than otherwise, I would have borne my part with you in this first brunt, were I not by strong necessity held back for the present. Make account of me, in the mean while, as of a man divided in myself with great pain, and as (natural bonds aside) having my better part with you." He enjoins to review their repentance; and to be careful and diligent in self-examination. "Sin being taken away by earnest repentance, and the pardon thereof from the Lord sealed up unto a man's conscience by His spirit, great shall be his security and peace in all dangers, sweet his comforts in all distresses, with happy deliverance from all evil, whether in life or in death."

"Next, after this heavenly peace with God and our own consciences, we are carefully to provide for peace with all men, what in us lieth, especially with our associates." . . . "In my own experience, few or none have been found which sooner give offence, than such as easily take it; neither have they ever proved sound and profitable members in society, which have nourished this touchy humor."

He warned them against private ends, "as a deadly plague." "As men are careful not to have a new house shaken with any violence, before it be well settled, and the parts firmly knit, so be you, I beseech you, brethren, much more careful that the house of God, which you are, and are to be, be not shaken with unnecessary novelties, or other oppositions at the first settling thereof." In the choice of governors he recommended them not to follow the "foolish multitude, who more honor the gay coat than either the virtuous mind of the man, or glorious ordinance of the Lord."

"These few things I do earnestly commend unto your care and conscience, joining therewith my daily incessant prayers unto the Lord, that He who hath made the heavens and the earth, the sea and all rivers of waters, and whose providence is over all His works, especially over all His dear children for good, would so guide and guard you in your ways, as inwardly by His spirit, so outwardly by the hand of His power, as that both you and we also, for and with you, may have after matter of praising His name all the days of your and our lives. Fare you well, in Him, in whom you trust and in whom I rest. An unfeigned well wisher of your happy success in this hopeful voyage."

XXI.

THE VOYAGE AND THE LANDING.

On the 5th of August, the *Mayflower* and the *Speedwell* left Southampton, pleasantly sailing in company down the river, past the beautiful shores of the Isle of Wight, and through the Needles to the open sea.

The Leyden Pilgrims, for the most part, were in the Speedwell, the rest of the company were better accommodated in the larger vessel. The mind of Cushman, for a time, seems to have been utterly broken down. He had fought the battle with conflicting parties, and been somewhat severely rebuked by his dissatisfied brethren, and now that matters were decided, he naturally felt the reaction. Every thing on board the Speedwell was uncomfortable; and the master of the ship, being under engagement to remain a year at the service of the Pilgrims, began to anticipate the effect of an inadequate supply of provisions.

The vessel sprung a-leak, and the passengers were

alarmed in consequence for their safety. It was deemed advisable to put into the romantic bay of Dartmouth, on the coast of Devonshire, for repairs (Aug. 13). Here, after they had rested four days, Cushman gave vent to his feelings in a letter to his friend, Edward Southwark, of Heneage House, Duke's Place, London: "Dartmouth, August 17. Loving friend, my most kind remembrance to you and your wife, with loving S. M. etc., whom in this world I never look to see again. For, besides the imminent dangers of this voyage, which are no less than deadly, an infirmity of body hath seized me, which will not in all likelihood leave me till death. What to call it I know not, but it is a bundle of lead, as it were, crushing my heart more and more these fourteen days, as that although I do the actions of a living man, yet I am but as dead; but the will of God be done." He then proceeds to give a melancholy account of the *Speedwell*. She would make no speed at all. "We lay at Hampton seven days, in fair weather, waiting for her, and now we be here waiting for her in as fair a wind as can blow, and so have done these four days, and are likely to lie four more, and by that time the wind will happily turn, as it did at Hampton." "She is open and leaky as a sieve." "If we had stayed at sea but three or four hours more, she would have sunk right down." In this deplorable state, we are not surprised that Cushman should take gloomy views of the enterprise. He had no idea, however, that Bradford would ever publish his letter. "Friend," he says, "if ever we make a plantation, God works a miracle; especially considering how scant we be of victuals." With the Psalmist he adds, in effect, "This is my infirmity." "Pass by my weak manner, for my head is weak, and my body feeble; the Lord make me strong in Him, and keep both you and yours."

Things were not improved when the ships sailed from Dartmouth. The disasters of the Speedwell compelled them to put in at Plymouth. It is pleasant to know that the Pilgrims received much kindness from Christian people there during the time of their detention. The *Speedwell* was again examined, and her ailment was pronounced to be that of a "general weakness." It was determined to prosecute the voyage with the *Mayflower* alone, and to give an opportunity for those who desired it to return. About twenty persons availed themselves of the option given. Some of these, however, had members of their family in the *Mayflower*, and went in the next ship, the *Fortune*, from London. The choice, to some extent, there is reason to suppose would be determined by the means they had of providing for themselves a home in England. Cushman, who never expected to see his friends in

London, must have surprised them by his early reappearance. He recovered from his heart complaint, and became a faithful and valuable helper afterwards.

Finally, the *Mayflower* left the shores of England, on the 6th of September, to encounter the terrible gales of the Atlantic with 101 passengers. Her condition was far from being sound. At one time one of the main braces of the ship gave way, and a serious consultation was entered into to consider whether they should go forward or return. A great iron screw, brought by the Pilgrims out of Holland, raised it to its place, and with a post under it, the cracked girder was set firm in the lower deck.

"Methinks I see it now, that one solitary, adventurous vessel, the *Mayflower* of a forlorn hope, freighted with the prospects of a future State, and bound across the unknown sea. I behold it pursuing, with a thousand misgivings, the uncertain, tedious voyage. Suns rise and set, and weeks and months pass, and winter surprises them on the deep, but brings them not the sight of the wished-for shore. I see them scantily supplied with provisions, crowded almost to suffocation in their ill-stored prison; delayed by calms; pursuing a circuitous route; and now driven in fury before the raging tempest, on the high and giddy waves. The awful voice of the storm howls through the rigging; the laboring masts seem straining from their base; the dismal sound of the pump is heard; the ship leaps, as it were, madly from billow to billow; the ocean breaks, and settles, with engulfing floods over the floating deck, and beats with deadening, shivering weight against the staggered vessel." *

Yet the fragile bark held on to the destined haven. On the 9th of November (the day after the battle of Prague), the storm-tossed Pilgrims first sighted land at Cape Cod. The prospect before them was cheerless in the extreme. Andrew Marvell wrote a poem, which some unacquainted with the "wild New England shore," suppose to have been descriptive of the landing of the Pilgrims. The following indicate its character:

> "He lands us on a grassy stage,
> Safe from the storm's and prelate's rage.
> He gave us the eternal spring,
> Which here enamels every thing;
> And sends the fowls to us in care,
> On daily visits through the air.
> He hangs in shades the orange bright,
> Like golden lamps in a green night;
> And does in the pomegranate close,
> Jewels more rich than Ormus shows.
> He makes the figs our mouths to meet;
> And throws the melons at our feet.
>   *   *   *   *   *

* Everett.

> "Thus sang they, in the English boat,
> A holy and a cheerful note;
> And all the way, to guide their chime,
> With falling oars they kept the time."

Far different was the desolate and wintry scene presented to the view of the Pilgrims. "Which way soever they turned their eye," says Bradford, "(save upward to the heavens,) they could have little solace or comfort in respect of any outward objects. For summer being done, all things stand upon them with a weather-beaten face; and the whole country, full of woods and thicket, represented a wild and savage hue."

To those who look for the first time upon the "weather-beaten face" of that dreary coast at such a season, Spring seems almost to be an impossibility. Certainly there was nothing inviting in natural scenery. "Not only the softer delights of pastoral loveliness, but those grander developments, which at least dignify nature in some of the severest manifestations of her infinite moods, were equally wanting. No awful and cloud-crowned mountain, luminous with perpetual snows, glittered upon their enchanted vision; no meadows before their eyes, enamelled with aramanthine flowers; no rivers, clearer and purer than the bountiful bosom of maternal earth ordinarily vouchsafes, sparkled between emerald banks and over golden sands; nor could they promise themselves to wander amidst consecrated groves, resonant with the intermingled harmonies of airy melodies, and loaded with the lingering odors of a myriad fragrant beds of spontaneous bloom beneath. But they saw before them the low swell of the yellow sand heap, and the dreariness of winter settling down in browner shadows upon the more distant hills; instead of the lustrous gleam that rolls with the under-current of the azure river, blending its blue to the gold, only the new-formed ice that glittered upon the margin of every standing pool,— for meads embroidered with luxuriant flowers of every softest tint or deeper dye, nothing but the level of the desolate marsh, stretching far away, crested only with its unsightly patches of ragged sedge, and for the lulling music of arcadian woods, no song but the solemn requiem of long-departed summer, breathed by the rising winds, in no gentle tones, to the responsive sighings of the November pines." *

And yet beneath the whole canopy of heaven, there was no spot more adapted to become the home of the pioneers of freedom, than the quiet and almost land-locked harbor within the bay to which the prow of the *Mayflower* was now turned. They expected, indeed, to have entered into the waters around the Island of Manhattan, beautiful as the

* Lunt.

Bay of Naples, and leading to the river Hudson, where the lovers of the picturesque may find as much to satisfy as on the Rhine at Coblentz, or in the majestic Rhone. But the Unseen Hand determined the course of the vessel to the destined haven.

Here they would find provision for their immediate wants in the fish and game, the supply of which was abundant. There were beautiful springs of water. They would find shelter from the stormy blast on the slope of the hills. The Indians had been reduced in number by the ravages of a plague some years before. With the untraversed continent on one side, and three thousand miles of ocean on the other, they were safe from the rage of persecution, and, at the same time, there was nothing to tempt the cupidity of men in quest of gain.

On the discovery of their position at Cape Cod, Bradford tells us, " after some deliberation had amongst themselves and with the master of the ship, they tacked about, and resolved to stand for the southward (the wind and weather being fair), to find some place about Hudson river for their habitation. But after they had sailed that course about half the day, they fell amongst dangerous shoals and breakers, and they were so far entangled therewith as they conceived themselves in great danger;[*]

---

[*] Twice the French made fruitless attempts to form a settlement at Cape Cod. De Monts, in 1605, with forty emigrants, came to this

and the wind shrinking upon them withal, they resolved to bear up again for the cape, and thought themselves happy to get out of those dangers before night overtook them, as by God's providence they did." "Being thus arrived in a good harbor and brought safe to land, they fell upon their knees, and blessed the God of heaven who had brought them over the vast and perilous ocean, and delivered them from all the perils and miseries thereof, again to set their feet on the firm and stable earth, their proper element."

On the 11th of November, in conformity with their original purpose to "form a body politic," and to suppress rising disaffection, the following constitution was adopted and signed in the cabin of the Mayflower:

"In the name of God, Amen.

"We, whose names are underwritten, the loyal subjects of our dread sovereign lord, King James, by the grace of God, of Great Britain, France, and Ireland, King, Defender of the Faith, etc., having

---

point, which they called Malebarre, but feared to land from the number of Indians. In 1606, Pourdrincourt, with Champlain, Champdore, renewed the colonizing effort. They were entangled among shoals, as soon as they came in sight of the cape, their rudder was broken, and they were obliged to anchor three leagues from the land. His men wantonly provoked a conflict with the natives. Lives were sacrificed on both sides, and the enterprise in consequence abandoned.

undertaken, for the glory of God and advancement of the Christian faith, and moreover of our king and country, a voyage, to plant the first colony in the northern parts of Virginia, do, by these presents, solemnly and mutually, in the presence of God and of one another, covenant and combine ourselves together into a civil body politic, for our better ordering and preservation, and furtherance of the end aforesaid, and by virtue hereof to enact, constitute, and frame, such just and equal laws, ordinances, acts, constitutions, and offices, from time to time, as shall be thought most meet and convenient for the general good of the colony; unto which we promise all due submission and obedience. In witness whereof we have hereunder subscribed our names, at Cape Cod, the 11th of November, in the year of the reign of our sovereign lord, King James of England, France, and Ireland, the eighteenth, and of Scotland the fifty-fourth, Anno Domini, 1620."

Bradford gives us to understand that the adoption of this famous compact was hastened from the mutinous speeches of strangers, who had joined their company. They said " when they came ashore they would use their own liberty; for none had power to command them, the patent they had being for Virginia and for New England, which belong to another government, with which the Virginia company had nothing to do." This excuse for rebellion was more ingenious than sound, for there still remained the obligations of morality, which are not confined within certain parallels of latitude. However, this act passed by the Pilgrim legislators was considered by them "as firm as any patent, and in some respects more sure."

Carver was chosen, or rather confirmed as governor for the year.

The " body politic," notwithstanding, were very much at the mercy of Mr. Jones, the master of the ship.

Indeed, there is reason to believe that he was chief of the mutineers. He and his company told the Pilgrims " that with speed they should look out a place with their shallop, where they would be at some near distance; for the season was such as he would not stir from thence, till a safe harbor was discovered by them where they would be, and he might go without danger; and that victuals consumed apace, but he must and would keep sufficient for themselves and their return. Yea, it was muttered by some, that if they got not a place in time, they would turn them and their goods ashore and leave them."

Unfortunately, the shallop was not in a fit state for the cruise of discovery, and the carpenter was such a bungler, that it took him six days to put it in repair. On the day the compact was signed, sixteen men were landed to explore the country. At night they returned with juniper wood as fuel, not having met with houses or inhabitants. Impatient of delay, some of the people volunteered to make a further exploration by land to find a place suitable for settlement. Their proposal was deemed to be too hazardous, but " seeing them resolute, they were permitted to go."

" Sixteen men were sent out, with every man his musket, sword, and corslet, under the conduct of Captain Miles Standish," with William Bradford, Stephen Hopkins, and Edward Tilley, to act as councillors. The party returned on the 17th of November, and announced their arrival, by firing their pieces. The longboat was put out, with Mr. Carver and Mr. Jones to receive them. They reported that they had seen a few Indians, and had met with springs of water and a heap of corn. The discovery of the corn they regarded as a special providence, as it supplied them with season the next year. They were careful afterwards to make the Indians full compensation. Some heaps of sand excited their curiosity. Digging into one of them they found a bow and arrows, as they supposed, " but," they say, " because we deemed them graves, we put in the bow again, and made it up as it was, and left the rest untouched, because we thought it would be odious unto them to ransack their sepulchres."

On the 27th of November, the shallop being repaired, a second expedition of thirty-four men staid for further discovery. In compliment for his "kindness and forwardness," Mr. Jones was appointed leader. Ten sailors were included in the foraging party. They had to wade to the shore, and on the first day and night were exposed to a violent snowstorm. They marched six or seven miles exposed to the bitter blast, and from the severity of which they found little protection at night. About eleven o'clock in the morning of the next day they rejoined the shallop, and sailed to what is now called Pamet river. Here they landed and traversed the country on its bank, some four or five miles. Night grew on, and the men were tired with marching up and down the steep hills and deep valleys (of Truro), which lay half a foot thick with snow. Some proposed to go further, but Mr. Jones, wearied with the excursion, preferred to take up their lodging. Under a few pine-trees they made their rendezvous, and enjoyed a splendid supper of "three fat geese and six ducks," having fasted all day.

After this indulgence they rather faltered in their resolution next morning, and, instead of tracing the river to its source, they went to look after the corn.

"Mr. Jones was earnest to go aboard." They sent him home with the sick and the weakest of their company, in charge of the corn. Eighteen remained on shore, having a strong desire "to make further discovery, and to find out the Indians' habitations."

They found, in the course of their wandering, a place covered with boards. "We mused," they tell us, "what it could be." Their curiosity got the better of a proper regard for the sanctity of the sepulchre, for it proved to be an Indian cemetery. Having once begun to dig, they did not stop until they had examined its contents. The trinkets, no doubt, stimulated their research. Some of the "prettiest things" they brought away, and then closed up carefully the mound. In the same spirit of adventure and curiosity, when ranging about, two of the sailors entered two deserted dwellings of the Indians, and brought away various curiosities. These transactions were by no means satisfactory, though they say they intended "to have brought some beads and other things to have left in the houses, in sign of peace, and that we meant to truck with them." In extenuation, it is only right to say that the first time they had an opportunity, they explained their object to the Indians, and gave them full satisfaction.

Resting awhile, after these expeditions, the Pilgrims then held a council, "what to do touching" their final place of abode. The "heart of winter" was upon them. The stores of provision were rapidly diminished, and Mr. Jones might again be restless. Some thought it best to abide at Cape Cod. Others suggested that a better place might be found, and in particular that they might find springs of water that would not be dried up in summer.

Robert Coppin, the pilot, told them a story " of a great navigable river and good harbor in the other headland of the bay (Manomet point), almost right over against Cape Cod, being in a right line not much above eight leagues distant, in which he had been once." On the 6th of December, ten of the Pilgrims, Captain Standish, Mr. Carver, William Bradford, Edward Winslow, John Tilley, Edward Tilley, John Howland, with Richard Warren, Stephen Hopkins and Edward Dotey (of London), and two of their own seamen, accompanied by two mates of the ship's company, Mr. Clarke and Mr. Coppen, the master gunner, and three sailors, launched from the ship in quest of a resting-place.

So extreme was the cold, that the spray of the sea, as it fell upon them, became ice, and gave them the appearance of men encased in glass. As they skirted along the coast they observed ten or twelve Indians, and tried to find a landing-place where they might avoid them. With great difficulty they got on shore late at night, and made themselves a barricade with logs and boughs, and appointed a sentinel to watch against the Indians, whose fires they observed in the distance. On the morning of the 7th of December, they divided their company, "some to coast along the shore in the boat, and the rest marched through the woods to see the land, if any fit place might be for their dwelling." "They ranged up and down all that day, but found no people nor any place they liked. When the sun grew low, they hasted out of the woods to meet with their shallop, to whom they made signs to come to them in a creek hard by, which they did at high-water." They were glad to meet, "for they had not seen each other all that day, since the morning." Erecting a barricade, as usual, they betook themselves to rest, for they were very weary. About midnight they were alarmed by a hideous yell. The sentinel called, "Arm! arm!" They stood to their arms, and "shot a couple of muskets, and then the noise ceased." "They concluded it was a company of wolves, for one of the seamen told them he had often heard such a noise in Newfoundland."

They rose at five in the morning, on the 8th of December, and continued in their prayers till daybreak. As they were preparing for breakfast and for further exploration — and some had carried their armor to the shore, and were returning — an unexpected and strange outcry was heard. One of the company being absent came running in, exclaimed "Indians! Indians!" on which the arrows came flying thickly among them. Captain Standish, having his piece in readiness, fired at the enemy; they rushed to arms, and returned the flight of arrows with a discharge of musketry. During this encounter, on the part of the infantry, there was a mimic naval engagement. The militant Pilgrims on shore called to their brethren in the shallop, "to know how it was with them." They answered, "Well! well!" every one, and "Be of good courage." "We heard," says the historian of the fight, "three of their pieces go off, and the rest called for a firebrand to light their matches. One took a log out of the fire on his shoulder, and went and carried it unto them; which was thought did not little discourage our enemies." The list of casualties happily was slight. "Some coats hung up in the barricado were shot through and through," but none of the Pilgrim army were hurt, and there is reason to hope that the Indians escaped equally without loss. A sachem, indeed, is supposed to have been wounded from the noise he made, but there is no certainty that his "extraordinary cry" arose from any shot having taken effect.

The Indians retreated, and the company under Miles Standish followed them very cautiously about a quarter of a mile. "Then," says the annalist, "we shouted all together two several times, and shot off a couple of muskets, and so returned. This we did that they might see we were not afraid of them nor discouraged." The Pilgrims gave thanks to God for their deliverance; gathered up a bundle of arrows to send to England, and in commemoration of the event called that place "the first encounter."

Sailing away from the scene of conflict, Bradford tells us "the wind was fair, and they coasted along (from Eastham to Manomet) about fifteen leagues; but saw neither river or creek to put into." In the afternoon the weather changed, the wind also, and the rain fell in torrents. The sea began to be rough, and the hinges of the rudder were broken. (They were nearing the mouth of Plymouth Bay.) Coppen the pilot said, " be of good cheer ! I see the harbor !" The shades of night gathered round them. The storm-tossed bark missed its course, and instead of entering Plymouth Bay was driven furiously toward a dangerous cove (between Gurnish Head and Saquish Point). The reliance of the crew is on the pilot, so he stands at the bows peering anxiously through the driving sleet at the wild and desolate shore, dimly visible. A terrific blast from the north strikes the boat, the mast is rent in three pieces, and the sail falls overboard, but the flood tide sweeps them on. In a fright the pilot exclaims, "The Lord be merciful unto us, I never saw that place before." A few minutes more and all may be lost. " About

with her," cries one of the sailors, " as you are men."
With all their might they strain the oars and wrench
the quivering vessel from the breakers.

"It was very dark, and rained sore, yet in the end
they got under the lee of a small island (Clarke's
Island), and remained there all night in safety."
They knew not that the place was an island until
morning. Some of their number hesitated to land
for fear of the Indians. The rest came on shore,
and with difficulty made a fire (all things being so
wet), and the rest were glad to come to them, for
after midnight the wind shifted to the north-west,
and it froze hard. But though it had been a day
and night of much trouble and danger unto them,
yet God gave them a morning of comfort and
refreshing (as usually he doth to his children), for
the next day was a fair sunshining day, and they
found themselves to be on an island secure from the
Indians, where they might dry their stuff, fix their
pieces, and rest themselves, and gave God thanks
for his mercies, in their manifold deliverances. And
this being the last day of the week, Dec. 9, they
prepared to keep the Sabbath.

On this Patmos of the New World, the Sabbath
(Dec. 10) dawned upon the Pilgrim leaders in peace
and in blessing.

The sacred day, since they left the shores of England, had been spent on board the *Mayflower*, but now, beneath the shelter of a gray rock, they met for worship.

That memorable rock still remains, situated near the ridge, on the eastern slope of the island. Its highest point, on the downhill side, is twelve feet from the ground. The western side slopes gradually toward the rising ground, easily accessible to the platform on the summit, which commands a view of the bay and its surrounding shores, the island lying in the midst, Gurnet and Manomet and the ocean beyond, and sometimes the far distant bluffs of Cape Cod. Here was the sentinel stationed, whilst the remainder of the party, shielded from the cold northerly and easterly winds by the rock, and on the west by the rise of the hill, lay safely under the warm southern lee.

Carver, Bradford, and Winslow, were well able to conduct the worship. The prayers they offered that day will yet receive their answers for many generations to come. They exhorted one another in the " sincerity of the gospel," and

> " Shook the depths of the deserts gloom,
> With their hymns of lofty cheer."

On Monday, the 11th of December, 1620, they sounded the harbor, and found it fit for shipping; and marched into the land, and found divers cornfields and little running brooks, a place (as they supposed) fit for situation; at least it was the best they could find, and the season and their present necessity made them glad to accept of it. So they returned to their ship again with this news to the rest of their people, which did much comfort their hearts.

On the 15th of December, they weighed anchor to go to the place they had discovered, and came within two leagues of it, but were fain to bear up again; but the 16th day the wind became fair, and they arrived safe in the harbor. And afterwards took better view of the place, and resolved where to pitch their dwelling. And the 25th day, began to erect the first house for common use (twenty feet square), " to receive them and their goods."

Their ranks were soon thinned by sickness and mortality. Bradford, Standish, Allerton, and Winslow, were all left widowers in the course of a few weeks. Six died in December; eight in January; seventeen in February; and thirteen in March. Fifty in all, out of 101, fell in the course of the winter. So many, that their graves were smoothed that the Indians might not count their number.

In the extremity of their distress, there were but "six or seven sound persons," who did " all the homely and necessary offices" for the sick. The "living were scarce able to bury the dead." The condition of the ship's crew was little better. Muskets could avail little at such a time as a protection against the Indians, yet, with the exception of the loss of tools, they suffered no injury from them. To their relief and surprise, Samoset, Sagamore of Pemaquid, came "boldly amongst them, and spoke to them in broken English, and told them of another Indian, called Squanto, who had been in London, in the employment of Mr. Slaney, and was brought back to his native country by Mr. Dermer." Through the spontaneous and kind intervention of Samoset, an important treaty of peace was made between Massasoit, the neighboring Indian chief, and the Pilgrims. Squanto gave them useful directions in preparing the ground for crops. On the return of spring, the Pilgrim settlers were a little revived. But they had renewed attacks of sickness, and their "common house" was burnt down. The ship would have left them, but for the enfeebled condition of the crew.

The captain, on the 5th of April, 1621, gave the command to return. The testing time was come, and the little colony of Plymouth stood firm. The church in the wilderness was formed, and not a man returned.

"Oh, strong hearts and true! not one went back in the *Mayflower*;
No, not one looked back who had set his hand to the ploughing!
Soon were heard on board the shouts and songs of the sailors,
Heaving the windlass round, and hoisting the ponderous anchor.

Then the yards were braced, and all sails set to the west wind,
Blowing steady and strong; and the *Mayflower* sailed from the harbor,
Rounding the point of the Gurnet, and leaving far to the southward,
Island and cape of sand, and the field of the First Encounter,
Took the wind on her quarter, and stood for the open Atlantic,
Borne on the send of the sea, and the swelling hearts of the Pilgrims.
Long in silence they watched the receding sail of the vessel
Much endeared to them all, as something living and human;
Then, as if filled with the Spirit, and wrapt in a vision prophetic,
Baring his hoary head, the excellent elder of Plymouth
Said, 'Let us pray,' and they prayed, and thanked the Lord and took courage.
Mournfully sobbed the waves at the base of the rock, and above them
Bowed and whispered the wheat on the hill of death; and their kindred
Seemed to awake in their graves, and to join in the prayer they uttered.
Sun-illumined and white, on the eastern verge of the ocean,
Gleamed the departing sail, like a marble slab in a graveyard;
Buried beneath it lay all hope of escaping."

It is beyond our present to trace the subsequent growth of the colony, notwithstanding the desertion of two thirds of the merchant adventurers, and their manifold vicissitudes and privations.

It remains for some other hand to trace the development of their principles in both hemispheres. For ten years they stood alone as the sentinels and pioneers of freedom in New England, reinforced in a few years by several brethren of a kindred spirit from the church at Southwark.

The testimony is borne by Captain John Smith, that they were the first to form a permanent and growing colony. Their success prepared the way for the larger colony of Massachusetts, and for all that followed.

A most extraordinary suggestion was made by one of the orators, on the day of laying the foundation stone of the monument at Plymouth, that a similar stone of memorial should be raised at Jamestown, in Virginia, in commemoration of the contemporary founders of a colony. If it were intended to record an admonitory inscription on such pillar of witness, the design might not be without utility, for the contrast between Plymouth Rock and Jamestown is striking and complete.

One of the gifted descendants of Governor Winthrop[*] has exhibited the difference between them in terms equally just and forcible.

"With the single exception that both emigrated from England, the colonies of Jamestown and Plymouth had nothing in common, and, to all outward appearances, the former enjoyed every advantage. The two companies, as it happened, though so long an interval elapsed between their reaching America, left their native land within about a year of each other; but under what widely different

[*] Hon. R. C. Winthrop, President of the Massachusetts Historical Society.

circumstances did they embark. The former set sail from the port of the metropolis, in a squadron of three vessels, under an experienced commander, under the patronage of a wealthy and powerful corporation, and with an ample patent from the crown. The latter betook themselves to their solitary bark, by stealth, under cover of the night, and, from a bleak and desert heath in Lincolnshire, while a band of armed horsemen, rushing down upon them before the embarkation was completed, made prisoners of all who were not already on board, and condemned husbands and wives, and parents and children to a hopeless separation. Nor did their respective arrivals on the American shores, though divided by a period of thirteen years, present a less signal contrast. The Virginia colony entered the harbor of Jamestown about the middle of May; and never could that lovely queen of spring have seemed lovelier, than when she put on her flowery kirtle and her wreath of clusters, to welcome those admiring strangers to the enjoyment of her luxuriant vegetation. There were no May flowers for the Pilgrims, save the name written, as in mockery, on the stern of their treacherous ship. They entered the harbor of Plymouth on the shortest day in the year, in this last quarter of December: and when could the rigid winter-king have looked more repulsive, than when, shrouded with snow and crowned with ice, he admitted those shivering wanderers within the realms of his dreary domination?

"But mark the sequel. From a soil teeming with every variety of production for food, for fragrance, for beauty, for profit, the Jamestown colonists reaped only disappointment, discord, wretchedness.

"Having failed in the great object of their adventure — the discovery of gold — they soon grew weary of their condition, and, within three years after their arrival, are found on the point of abandoning the country. Indeed, they are already embarked, one and all, with this intent, and are already at the mouth of the river, when, falling in with new hands and fresh supplies, which have been sent to their relief, they are induced to return once more to their deserted village.

"But even up to the very year in which the Pilgrims landed, ten years after this renewal of their designs, they 'had hardly become settled in their minds,' had hardly abandoned the purpose of ultimately returning to England. And their condition may be illustrated by the fact, that in 1619, and again in 1621, cargoes of young women (a commodity of which there was scarcely a sample in the whole plantation, and would to God, that all the traffic in human flesh on the Virginia coast, even at this early period had been as innocent in itself and beneficial in its results) were sent out by the corpoporation in London, and sold to the planters for wives, at from one hundred and twenty to one hundred and fifty pounds of tobacco apiece!

"Nor was the political condition of the Jamestown colony much in advance of its social state. The charter, under which they came out, contained not a single element of popular liberty, and secured not a single right or franchise to those who lived under it. And, though a gleam of freedom seemed to dawn upon them in 1619, when they instituted a colonial assembly, and introduced the representative system for the first time into the New World, the precarious character of their popular institutions, and the slender foundation of their popular liberties at a much later period, even as far down as 1671, may be understood from that extraordinary declaration of Sir William Berkely, then Governor of Virginia, to the Lords commissioners: 'I thank God, there are no free schools nor printing, and I hope we shall not have these hundred years! for learning has brought disobedience, and heresy and sects into the world; and printing has divulged them, and libels against the best government. God keep us from both.'

"But how was it with the Pilgrims? From a soil of comparative barrenness they gathered a rich harvest of contentment, harmony, and happiness. Coming to it for no purpose of commerce or adventure, they found all that they sought — *religious freedom* — and that made the wilderness to them like Eden, and the desert as the garden of the Lord.

"Of quitting it, from the very hour of their arrival, they seem never once to have entertained, or even conceived, a thought. The first foot that leaped gently, but fearlessly, on Plymouth Rock, was a pledge that there would be no retreating, — tradition tells us, that it was the foot of MARY CHILTON. They have brought their wives and their little ones with them, and what other assurance could they give that they have come to their *home?* And accordingly they proceed at once to invest it with all the attributes of home, and to make it a free and happy home.

"The compact of their own adoption under which they landed, remained the sole guide of their government for nine years, and though it was then superseded by a charter from the corporation within whose limits they had fallen, it was a charter of a liberal and comprehensive character, and under its provisions they continued to lay broad and deep the foundations of civil freedom.

"But," continues Mr. Winthrop, "the Virginia type was not complete, when it first appeared on the coast of Jamestown. . . . . The year 1620 was unquestionably the great epoch of American destinies. Within its latter half were included the two events which have exercised incomparably the most controlling influence on the character and fortunes of our country. At the very time the Mayflower, with its precious burden, was engaged in its perilous voyage to Plymouth, another ship, far otherwise laden, was approaching the harbor of Virginia. It was a Dutch man-of-war, and its cargo consisted of *twenty slaves*, which were subjected to slavery on their arrival, and with which the foundations of domestic slavery in North America were laid.

"I see those two fate-freighted vessels, laboring under the divided destinies of the same nation, and striving against the billows of the same sea, like the principles of good and evil advancing side by side on the same great ocean of life. I hear from the one the sighs of wretchedness, the groans of despair, the curses and clankings of struggling captivity, sounding and swelling on the same gale, which bears only from the other the pleasant voices of prayer and praise, the cheerful melody of contentment and happiness, the glad, the glorious anthem of the free."

The contrast between Plymouth and Jamestown might be illustrated by other facts and incidents, but we will not add to the eloquent words of this gifted New Englander, to whom the honor properly belongs of defending the honor of the Pilgrims.

Our object throughout, in the historical sketch

now coming to a close, has been rather to show the course of the Pilgrims and of their precursors, in their character as "witnesses." We are reminded, by their early trials and by their distinct separation as a people, as well as in their subsequent wanderings and vicissitudes, of the history of God's ancient witnessing people. The truth, destined for universal diffusion for ages, was "kept secret," intrusted to the care of a people few in number, almost unknown, or known only to be despised, but the time for its manifestation came in the unfailing purpose of Him who seeth the end from the beginning.

The martyrs of Southwark were strongly impressed with the conviction that the truth "made known to them," was to be held by them in trust, not only for the people of their own time, but also for coming generations.

In the lowest extremity of weakness and of trial, in the cell, and when standing on the gibbet, they made their appeal to posterity. For a moment they seem never to have lost confidence in the ultimate triumph of their principles. We have seen, in the review of their course, how closely the Pilgrims followed the footsteps of the martyrs.

Amidst their cares in Holland, they did not forget their obligations as stewards of the manifold grace of God, in relation to the truth they had received.

They might have contented themselves with the formalities of worship, without continuing the discussion of their views of church government. It is possible that, by the prudential reserve recommended to them by Junius, their exile might have afforded opportunities for the acquisition of wealth, and that when the agitation of the original controversy had passed from memory, they might have quietly returned to their own land. But they did not "keep silence." Not that they kept up an unreasoning clamor, for their testimony was as remarkable for its clearness and strength as for its persistence. The argument, conducted by Robinson at Leyden, with so much calmness and force against opponents of every order, shows the fulness of their conviction.

After their landing at Plymouth, it might have been supposed that in the rigors of the winter, their constant exposure to the Indians, and the incessant toil necessary to provide for themselves accommodations, and to meet their heavy payments to the adventurers, their zeal for the maintenance of their principles would be abated. What scope, it might have been said, can they find for agitation within bounds so narrow, at such a distance from civilization, and without the use of the printing-press?

Whether ruined or successful colonists, the natural expectation would be that they must be collapsed as congregationalists. The event proved otherwise.

The labors of the Pilgrims were indeed severe,— they were wasted by sickness occasioned by bodily want and constant exposure, their graves were more numerous in the first winter than their dwellings; nevertheless they kept continually in mind the service required of them in fidelity to the truth. They found time, after returning from the toil of the day in the field or in the fishing-boats, to pursue their theological studies. In the Boston Athenæum may be found a splendid folio copy of one of the Greek Fathers, inscribed with the name of William Brewster. The care with which it was preserved with the other volumes of his library, may indicate to us something of the intellectual habits of the Pilgrim leaders. Brewster was a layman, and had spent the greater part of his life in the service of the State, in various capacities, yet a glance at his collection of books will show the order of his mind. Here are the works of Beza, Musculus, Peter Martyr, Erasmus, Calvin, Chrysostom, Piscator, Stephanus, Scultetus, Pareus, and Molerinus. Besides Greek and Latin authors, we find the "masterpieces" of English theologians, with polemic works on the Reformation and Protestant nonconformity, church history, moral and political philosophy, and books of practical utility on general topics. The Pilgrims knew their ground, and they held it with intelligence and firmness never surpassed.

Governor Bradford, whilst occupied in recording the incidents of the eventful course, did not neglect to acquaint himself with their church principles. He took his full share in expounding them to the young people of the colony. Deacon Fuller was not less conversant with the truth for which they had suffered. The influence exerted by his example and conversation on the minds of the Puritan settlers, who followed the Pilgrims into the wilderness, we learn from the letter of Endicot, dated Namkeak, May 11, 1629: "I acknowledge myself," he says, "much bound to you for your kind love and care in sending Mr. Fuller amongst us, and rejoice much that I am by him satisfied touching your judgment of the outward form of God's worship; it is, as far as I can gather, no other than is warranted by the evidence of truth."

The effect of the Pilgrim testimony was not confined within their own borders. The Puritan settlers, in writing to their brethren in England, had to speak uniformly of their candor and kindness. They held the truth firmly, but in the spirit of meekness and charity, and the impression produced was greatly enhanced by the combination. Historical investigation, when carried to the close of the seventeenth century, will show the constant progress of the "leaven" of their principles. Milton was not a stranger to the course of the Pilgrim Fathers.

He was not insensible to the loss sustained by England from their expatriation. "What numbers," he said, "of faithful and free-born Englishmen and good Christians have been constrained to forsake their dearest home, their friends and kindred, whom nothing, but the wide ocean and the savage deserts of America, could hide and shelter from the fury of the bishops. Oh, if we could but see the shape of our dear Mother England, as poets are wont to give a personal form to whom they please, how would she appear, think ye, but in a mourning weed, with ashes upon her head, and tears abundantly flowing from her eyes; to behold so many of her children exposed at once, and thrust from things of dearest necessity, because their conscience could not assent to things which the bishops thought indifferent?

"Let the astrologers be dismayed at the portentous blaze of comets and impressions in the air, as foretelling troubles and changes to states; I shall believe there cannot be a more ill-boding sign to a nation (God turn the omen from us!) than when the inhabitants, to avoid insufferable grievances at home, are enforced by heaps to leave their native country."

The loss to England by the banishment of the best and most devoted of her sons, undoubtedly was great, and to this day it is felt in all her dependencies, but it was a gain to humanity.

The Pilgrims were saved by their catholicity of spirit, and by the expansiveness of their views and affections. They did not pine around the rock of Plymouth in wretchedness and discontent. They did not pour forth bitter complaints, or sigh out their strength in unavailing regrets. Though they were not mindful to return to the land of their birth, they did not cease to love it, and to desire its highest and lasting welfare. The unpublished dialogue, written by Governor Bradford, on "Popery, Episcopacy, Presbyterianism, and Independency," affords important evidence of their noble and generous sentiments. We quote one or two passages for the sake of illustration:

"For the fruits of the congregational discipline, say the 'ancient men' to the 'young men,' as it hath been exercised amongst us, Mr. Cotton saith, though in much weakness, the Lord hath not left us without testimony from heaven.

"First, in making these churches a little sanctuary to many thousands of his servants, who fled over hither to avoid the unsupportable pressures of their consciences by the episcopal tyranny. Secondly, in blessing the ministry of our preaching here with like fruits of conversion, as in our native country, of sundry both elder and younger persons who came over hither, not out of conscience, but out of respect to friends or outward enlargements, but have here

found that grace which they sought not after. . . . .
Fourthly, it hath been also a testimony from heaven of God's blessing upon our way, that many thousands in England, in all quarters of the kingdom, have been awakened to consider the causes of church discipline, for which we have suffered this hazardous and voluntary banishment into this remote wilderness, and have therefore by letters conferred with us about it.

"Of their love and loyalty, see what Mr. Barton writeth and affirmeth against Mr. Prynne: 'We dare,' saith he, 'challenge the world in point of fidelity to the state and our native country. Who do pray more frequently for them? So that herein you cannot say, we are Independents.

"'As for want of love, and that of the best kind, to the public cause and that state, we are ready to help and serve it with our best abilities. And for true charitableness, brother,' saith he, 'Where is it to be found if not in those churches you call Independent? But you say that our love is among ourselves (and God grant it may ever be so), yet it ends not there, but extends to all. And, brother, for a close,' saith he, 'I challenge you to show me one parochial congregation in England wherein there is, or can be, the like love one to another; the like care one for another; the like union and communion of members in one mystical body, in a sympathy of affections in such a fraternity as is described in Ps. cxxxiii., a lively type of a true church of Christ.

"YOUNG MEN.

" These are blessed fruits, and happy are those churches in which they may be found and wherein they continue and abide. These are of the Lord's planting, and are not to be found in every garden. The Lord purge and prune his churches, and water them with the dew of heaven, that they may continue to bring forth fruit unto Him, that we may enjoy a part in this blessing in our days.

"ANCIENT MEN.

" We have the rather noted these things that you may see the worth of these things, and not negligently lose what your fathers have obtained with so much hardship, but maintain these privileges, which not man, but the Lord Jesus the King of the church hath purchased for you. You see how, when they were lost in the former ages, both what evil and what misery followed thereupon, and how long, and with what difficulty it was before they could, in any purity, be recovered again. They were lost by sloth and security in the people, and by pride and ambition in the bishops and elders. But it hath cost much blood and sweat in the recovery, and will do no less care and pains in the keeping of them. It will require much prayer, zeal, holiness, humility, vigilancy and love, and peace, with a spirit of meekness, that liberty be not abused, and by pride and faction turned into licentiousness. 'Stand fast in the liberty,' saith the apostle, 'wherein Christ hath made us free.' Ye have been called into liberty, only use not liberty for an occasion to the flesh, but by love serve one another."

The spectacle presented in the social condition of America in our own time, is one by which no thoughtful mind can be unimpressed. The germ of the evil, conveyed in the Dutch ship to Jamestown in 1620, has been developed in gigantic proportions. England long fostered its growth, until it became rank and prolific. The good seed sown in weakness, in obscurity, and with many tears, has also yielded abundant fruit. To speak without metaphor, the descendants of the Pilgrims have advanced, by successive migrations, in a line extending from the Atlantic coast toward the shores of the Pacific. Their onward course has excited little attention in comparison with the march of armies. A row of wagons, with a few oxen, driven slowly because of the mothers and the children, on their winding way to the distant settlement; the sound of the axe in the first clearance, the curling smoke rising from the log cabins at the edge of the pine forest, or in the boundless prairie, these are the external signs of advancing civilization. They are followed by cultivated fields, smiling villages, and populous cities, but the world knows little of the process by which the mighty change is produced. It is a fact, nevertheless, at once grand and delightful, that before the sons of New England, holding fast the principles of their Pilgrim ancestry, slavery of every form constantly recedes, and that communities are called into existence, enjoying in the highest degree the blessings of order and of peace. Everywhere the church and the school-house mark the character of the settlement, and the spirit of the men by whom it is formed.

Well is it understood by such men, that the gospel is the only guaranty for the security and freedom of the natives. They thoroughly comprehend that secular education alone can never give the self-control and the expansive social sympathies essential for the preservation of liberty. Hence their deep and growing concern for the evangelization of the mighty West.

"No more," says Mr. Beecher, "shall the voice be heard saying, 'Go ye into all the world,' but the sound has never ceased to echo. Every groan of the slave is its echo; every wail of sorrow is its echo; every petition from isle or idolatrous continent, every revolution invokes you; every uprising of man, struggling for the liberty of manhood and the equality of civilization is an invocation. But amid all these sounds there comes one louder, deeper, and more earnest. Is it the wind that comes to our ears sighing across the prairie? It is the voice of our kindred that dwell there. Is that the roar of the forest, or the breaking of the lakes upon the shore? It is the sound of the multitudes, loud as many waters or as mighty thunderings. It rolls from the vast basin of the Mississippi, along the far travelling Missouri, and from the mountains whose snows it drinks, and over them from the shores of the Oregon. It is the Pacific calling to the Atlantic, *deep calling unto deep.* The multitudinous dwellers between those shores are our kindred. We taught them to speak. For us they yearn at eventide. For us they sigh when fever-scorched, and turning to the the East, with devotion fonder than the oriental, they call for father and mother! names, in this land, next in love and sanctity to the name of God. When that solemn invocation falls upon the East without answer, her days will be numbered. But it shall not be unheeded. O thou mighty West, I who have known and loved thee, cry back again our whole-souled sympathy! For thee we will pray, for thee shall go forth our institutions. Unto thee shall go forth our sons and our daughters. Thy destiny shall be our destiny. Thy glory our glory."

Elevated as is the feeling and purpose expressed in these glowing words, those who have received in trust the principles for which our fathers suffered, must ascend to a higher point, and their vision must extend to a wider horizon. The prairies are vast, but our field is the world.

It is time to renew the testimony of the Pilgrims, — the testimony for purity of communion, the equality of Christian brethren, and freedom of worship. The best hopes of humanity are bound up in these principles. Ignorance of them has been the occasion of oppression, conflict, and suffering for ages.

The stability and moral force, existing in the Anglo - Saxon race of both hemispheres, may be attributed mainly to the character formed directly or indirectly by these principles. The position occupied by the two countries is one of powerful influence. There is no need to institute invidious comparisons as to the extent of that influence. But it may be observed that the younger branch of the family has sent forth its missionaries to the primal seats of civilization. The descendants of the Pilgrims are building up the old waste places, the ruins of many generations in the regions of Tyre, Nineveh, and Babylon. They are lighting again the lamps of the seven churches, and they are the more welcome in those eastern lands, because they are not entangled in the political relations of the Old World.

But there is an opportunity for the friends of truth and freedom, in England and America, to unite in the reiteration of their testimony.

The difficulties in the way of this combined action are not to be overlooked. The proposal to erect a Pillar of Witness in Southwark, was not hailed in the old country with enthusiasm. There were some who, instead of bringing a stone to the wall as the tribute of gratitude, would prefer to cast a stone at the builders. It must be admitted, however reluctantly, that many who from habit, parental example, and early associations, are connected with nonconformist churches in England, have little or no acquaintance with the history of their origin, or of the influence exerted by them.

How can we expect ardor in an object which is not understood?

The attempt to secure, in the place where our martyrs suffered, a spot of ground where American brethren might stand in England as firmly as on Plymouth Rock, did not commend itself to all. There are some who would rather keep alive the "old hatred" and increase the estrangement. The erection of a memorial building, in which the descendants of the Pilgrims might meet in love and peace beneath the same roof, was not an object to find favor with such persons. From such causes the work has been hindered, and after the care, anxiety, and toil of nine years, on the part of a few people in Southwark, the building remains to-day as a fragment.

In the tenth year of their sojourn at Plymouth, the Pilgrims hailed the arrival of the leaders of the Massachusetts colony. They stood firmly at their post until the succor came, which secured the possession of the American continent. Will the tenth year of our patient toil in Southwark, witness the reinforcement that will determine successfully the issue we have sought so long?

Nine years ago the Hon. Abbott Lawrence addressed to the pastor of the church of the Pilgrim Fathers in Southwark, the following deeply interesting letter:

"138 PICCADILLY, LONDON, 22d April, 1851.

"DEAR SIR, — I have read with much pleasure the papers you were kind enough to send me, respecting the efforts you are now making to erect a Congregational church to the memory of the Pilgrim Fathers. In common with most of my countrymen, I entertain the most profound and sincere reverence for the memory of the band of heroic Christians, who, in the face, in the Old World, of neglect, if not of oppression, and, in the New, of terrific trials, of countless dangers, of death from cold, from starvation, and from a treacherous foe, founded a Christian colony, which has now grown into one of the great nations of the earth. If that nation has proved to the world that religious freedom and religious faith may flourish together, or that perfect liberty and perfect law are not incompatible, I attribute it, in no slight degree, to the deep and permanent influence which the principles of Brewster and Robinson, Carver and Bradford, and their little commonwealth, have had upon its character.

"It seems superfluous to speak of this little community of men and women (*noble women*, too), which has now become one of the admirations of the world, and which gathered within its ranks as great, I believe, if not a greater, an amount of Christian faith, fortitude, endurance, and hope, than was ever found of equal numbers on earth. The 'Rock of Plymouth,' where they finally made their home, has become our Mecca, to which we annually, on the wintry anniversary of their landing, make a pilgrimage, to renew our vows of fidelity to the principles of our forefathers, and offer up our thankful devotions to their and our God for the civil and religious liberty He has permitted us to inherit from them. Long may that rock remain, — a monument to teach my countrymen so to conduct the affairs of the present, that the future may not be unworthy of the past we have received.

"The influence of their example is not confined to the land where it was displayed. *Europe has begun to study their principles;* and I think I see their influence increasing in this country. I am proud when I see efforts, like the present, to extend among the British people a just knowledge of these English men and women. You, too, may well be proud to be the pastor of a church where they preached and worshipped, and may appeal without fear to our brethren, both in England and throughout the world, to come forward and erect a church in commemoration of an event, the effects of which, already deeply felt, are destined probably to influence the world more than any other in modern history.

"With my most sincere wishes for your complete success in your interesting undertaking, I am, dear sir, very faithfully, your obedient servant,

"ABBOTT LAWRENCE."

No one better knew than Mr. Lawrence the nature of the obstacles to be overcome on English ground in such an undertaking. It was his purpose, on his return to America, to bring the subject prominently before the New England societies, but the changes of the time, and the event of his deeply lamented death, prevented the fulfilment of his design.

The pen must be restrained in reference to matters of private interest, but, in the event of the ultimate accomplishment of the object, it should be known to all who are specially concerned, that but for the magnificent kindness of Mrs. Lawrence, the feeble hands into which the undertaking fell must have relinquished their grasp. From personal regard to the memory of the Pilgrims, and with relative sympathy, kindred with that of Lady Franklin in another object, Mrs. Lawrence gave the timely aid which prevented the defeat of a purpose rendered so sacred in her estimation, by the letter just quoted.

There are signs that the facts connected with the advancement of the principles of the Pilgrims, in the land of their adoption, will command greater attention in Europe. It is a significant circumstance that one of the first paintings, prepared to illustrate English history, for the Palace at Westminster, is that of the embarkation of the Pilgrim Fathers. The selection of subjects was made by a committee of which Lord Macaulay was principal adviser. In deference to prejudice, likely to be excited by too bold a step, the title of the picture was for a long time withheld, and another designation given less startling to aristocratic observers. But now the true description is given, and the Pilgrim Fathers are as prominent in the British houses of Parliament as at the capitol of Washington. The British nation is being put under an educational process on the subject. Inquiry is excited, and, with patient perseverance for a few years, no one in England will again make the mistake of confounding the Pilgrim Fathers with the fathers of the Romish church.

The form in which the testimony is given is one that rivets the attention of young persons, and awakens the finest sympathies. The story of martyrdom, and of exile in connection with the founding of a vast and powerful nation, cannot be listened to and understood to be again forgotten.

The remembrance of it for life lends a peculiar, though it may be, unconscious influence in the formation of character. Those who are associated with churches of the same faith and order, no longer confine their view to the particular society of which they are personally members. They think of their brethren in other lands, as laboring for the advancement of a cause, which events have shown to be identified with the freedom and stability of nations. It is a hopeful circumstance that both in England and in America there are men of high standing in society, who are alive to the importance of diffusing the knowledge of this remarkable history.

A better acquaintance with the facts recorded in these pages, only a quarter of a century ago, would have saved English colonists in Australia, and in other parts of the globe, from serious hinderances and severe struggles which have too much retarded their progress. What, again, would be the advantage if the priest-ridden nations of Europe could once understand that religion is not intended to be an instrument in the hands of despots for the enslavement of mankind? Wearied with the yoke of Rome, Italy knows not as yet how churches may be free, and that the "household of faith" may exist with as much safety to the state, as the domestic constitution. It is possible to communicate this knowledge in a manner that will at once instruct and delight. The materials are being collected, and, in the plain and unadorned narrative we have given, some facts may be found to add in their degree to the common store. The genius and the eloquence of New England have always been tributary to the work of diffusing this kind of knowledge. It is a satisfaction to be assured that, whatever may be the issue as to the completion of the memorial church at Southwark, every incident brought to light in these pages will become as familiar to the descendants of the Pilgrims as they are to the mind of the writer. They will form in part the text of the historian, the orator, and the poet. In the pleasant homes of the Northern States, the abodes of intelligence, of Christian virtue, and of sanctified affection, and in the far West, where the Sabbaths of New England are not forgotten, the names of Richard Fitz, Henry Barrowe, John Greenwood, John Penry, Francis Johnson, Henry Jacob, and John Smyth, will be linked with the precious memories of John Robinson, William Brewster, William Bradford, and the rest of the Pilgrim band.

The time will come when, in England, it shall be known as familiarly, notwithstanding the haze of national vanity or prejudice, and the blending influence of political contentions, that there are myriads, severed from us by the Atlantic, who speak our language, hold our faith, observe our simple form of Christian worship, and cherish the spirit of freedom in a degree not excelled by any order of men on the face of the world besides.

Slowly this international and mutually fraternal acquaintance may be ripened. Many, who long to witness its happy results, may go down to the sepulchre, as " our friend " who sleeps in peace on Mount Auburn, before the dawn of that happy day. But every kind word, every generous act, every fervent prayer, will hasten the event.

Would that Christians in England, and in particular those of the Congregational order, could know, as does the writer of these lines, how amiable, how zealous, how affectionate and devout, are their transatlantic brethren in circles apart from the tumult and distraction of public life. It would enrich the memory of the heart, and give them new and more delightful anticipations of the heavenly state. They would be refreshed and animated by the continual recurrence of scenes and incidents, both of the home and of the sanctuary, the most grateful; and entertain, in consequence, firmer and brighter hopes for the whole race of man. But it is enough. The Great Peacemaker will reconcile all things in heaven and in earth. In Him all the families of the earth shall be blessed. A little longer, and the redeemed of all nations shall meet in their final home. There shall be one fold and one shepherd.

INDEX.

	PAGE
AINSWORTH, Henry, pastor of Amsterdam church	134
AMERICA, early plans for settling	109
AMSTERDAM, Pilgrims form a church in	134
divisions in church at	163
order of worship in church at	164
BACON, Lord, opinion of the Brownists	184
BARROWE, Henry, visits Greenwood in prison	54
flung into prison	56
writings of in prison	57
examined by Andros and Hutchinson	66
indicted for non-conformity	78
letter to "a countess," entire	78
proposes a conference with the bishops	91
execution of	95
BELLOT, Scipio, arrested for publishing	78
pleads for a conference	93
dies in prison	132
BERNARD, Richard, forms an "inner church"	161
BOWLAND, Thomas, deacon of first Separatist church	16
BRADFORD, William, early life of	142
character of	283
unpublished dialogue of, quoted	285
"BRETHREN of the second separation," why so called	137
BREWER, Thomas, patron of the Pilgrim printing-office	167, 210
imprisoned by the Leyden University	212
trial of, for printing	215
decides to go to England	221
returns to Leyden, and again to England	226
imprisoned and liberated	226

INDEX.

BREWSTER, William, receives the Scrooby church . . 141
    sketch of 142
    previously acquainted in Holland 162
    Pilgrim printer in Leyden 162, 210
    attempts to arrest 211
    library of, in Boston Athenæum 282
BROWN, John, chaplain of Duchess of Suffolk . . . 27
BROWNE, Robert, definition of a church 30
    silenced 32
    source of the name "Brownist" , . . . 32, 41
    apostasy of 32, 41, 68
BROWNISTS, why the Separatists called . . . 32, 243
BUCK, David, imprisoned, and discussion with Francis Johnson 125

CANADA, ancient boundaries of 114
CAPE COD, Pilgrims arrive at 255
    French attempts to settle 258
CARTWRIGHT'S controversy with Mrs. Stubbs . . 34
CARVER, John, delegate to the Virginia company . . 201
    deacon of the Leyden church 206
    elected first governor of the Pilgrims . . . 260
CHURCH, first Separatist formed 16
    Robert Browne's definition of 30
    "in the house" 51
    formed at Rochford 52
    Barrowe's and Greenwood's definition of . . 59
    formed in Amsterdam 134
    Robinson's view of 176
    Arthur Hildersham's definition of . . . 186
    Henry Jacob's definition of 187
    formed in Southwark 188
CHURCHMAN, Mrs. Mary, experience of . . . 148
CLARK'S ISLAND, the landing upon 269
CLERK, John, reason of arrest of 183
CLIFTON, Richard, joins the Separatists . . . 139
    first pastor of the Scrooby church . . . 141
    retires to Holland 163
COMPACT of the Pilgrims in the Mayflower . . 259
CONFORMITY, mode of enforcing by Elizabeth . . 3
              by James I. . . 144
              extreme . . . 183

INDEX.   303

COPPIN, Robert, pilot of the Mayflower	265
COPPING, John, arrested and executed	31
CUSHMAN, delegate to the Virginia company	201
negotiations of, for a patent	228
agreement of, with the Merchant Adventurers	234
Pilgrim protest against the agreement of	235
Robinson's testimony to character of	235
letter of, to Edward Southwark	252
leaves the Mayflower at Plymouth, England	254
DEACONS, the first of Southwark church	73
DENNIS William, a martyr	32
ELIZABETH, effect of the accession of	3
feelings at the death of Barrowe and Greenwood	96
FIRST house built in Plymouth	271
Sabbath, spent on Clark's Island	269
Separatist church in England	16
first pastor of	16
members of	19
FITZ, Richard, first Separatist pastor	16
death of, in prison	78
FULLER, deacon of Leyden church, influence of	283
GAINSBORO church in two bands	141
GREENWOOD, John, first mention of	52
imprisoned	54
interview with Barrowe	55
writings of	57
conference of, with Hutchinson	64
chosen teacher of Southwark church	72
execution of	95
Elizabeth's opinion of	96
GRINDAL's letter to Cecil	11
to Bullinger	14
HAMPTON COURT conference	144
HILDERSHAM, the Puritan leader, imprisoned	186
HUDSON, Henry, voyages and discoveries of	196

JACOB, Henry, discussion of, with Francis Johnson . . . 126
  petition of, to King James 143
  imprisoned 145
  withdraws to Holland 146
  returns to England 183
  letter of, to Southwark church 185
  reorganizes the church in Southwark . . 187, 190
  chosen pastor of " " . . . 188
  character of 190
  migrates to New England 191
  death and burial of, unknown 191
JAMES I. raises the hopes of the Puritans 143
  proclaims conformity 144
  measures of, for enforcing conformity 183
  attempts of, to suppress the Holland Pilgrims . . 193
JOHNSON, Francis, account of conversion of 72
  chosen pastor of Southwark church 73
  letter of, to Lord Burghley 116
  imprisoned 117
  petition of his father for 122
  discussion of, with Henry Jacob 125
  banished to Newfoundland 131
  pastor of church in Amsterdam . . . 134, 163
  petition of, to the king for a return to England . . 182
JONES, master of the Mayflower 261
  threats of, to the Pilgrims 261

LAWRENCE, Hon. Abbott, letter of, to the Memorial church . 293
LAY INDEPENDENTS, the early 13
LETTER of Abbot Lawrence to the author 293
  Archbishop Parker and Bishop Grindal to Cecil . 8, 11
  Attorney-General to the Lord Keeper . . . 93
  Barrowe to "a countess" 78
  the bishops on visiting the imprisoned Separatists . 62
  Cushman to Edward Southwark 252
    to Robinson 236
  Dudley Carleton on the arrest of Brewster 211–220
  Francis Johnson to Lord Burghley . 116, 120
  Henry Jacob to the Bishop of London . . 145
    to the Southwark church . . 185
  John Smyth to the Scrooby church . . . 142

INDEX.

LETTER of Penry to his wife 98
        to the church 102
        Phillips on the death of Barrowe and Greenwood . 95
        the Pilgrims to Sir John Worstenholme . . 204
        Robinson and Brewster to Sir Edwin Sandys . . 206
            to Carver 235
            and Carver to the Pilgrims . . . 248
        Thomas Lever to Bullinger 4
        William Whittingham 6
            White to Edward Deering . . . 23
            Zouche to Carleton 222
LEVER, Thomas, letter of, to Bullinger 4
LEYDEN, migration of Pilgrims to 166
    articles of church in, to Council of England . . 201
LORD'S SUPPER by the Southwark church 74

MARTYRS, names of Separatist . . . 13, 17, 31, 76, 95, 108
MAYFLOWER, hired by Cushman 237
    Clark hired as pilot of 238
    sailing of, from the Thames to Southampton . . 240
            Southampton 251
            Dartmouth 252
            Plymouth 254
    arrival of, at Cape Cod 255
            Plymouth 271
    return of, to England 272
MEMORIAL CHURCH in Southwark 191
    progress of building a 292

ORDINATION of the first officers of the church . . . 71

PASTOR, how to be elected 60
PATENT, negotiations of Carver and Cushman for . . . 228
    obtained from the Virginia company . . . 233
    terms of, obtained from Virginia company useless . 234
PENRY, John, sketch of 73
    letter of, to his wife 98
    first suggests migration to America 107
    execution of 108
PERKINS, William, counsel of, to Robinson . . . 168

PILGRIMS, failure of first attempts of, to reach Holland . . 156
    imprisoned for attempts to flee 157
    separation of, from wives and children 158
    reasons of, for removing to Holland . . . 160, 193
    removal of, to Leyden 166
    occupation of, in Leyden 167
    debates of, on migrating to America 196
    negotiations of, with the Virginia company . . . 201
    belonging to London 203
    appoint a fast 208
    obtain a patent in the name of John Wincob . . 233
    slender means of 238, 247
    leave Leyden 244
    debark from Delft Haven 245
    arrive at Southampton 246
    part of, separate for London, ... 253
    final departure of, from England 254
    first see Cape Cod 255
    compact of, signed 259
    exploring parties of 262, 263, 265
    "First Encounter" of, with Indians . . . 267
    first Sabbath of, in New World 269
    land at Plymouth 270
    build their first house 271
    form a treaty with Massasoit 272
    contrasted with the Jamestown colony . . . 274
    testimony to the character of 283
    present repute of, in England 296
PURITANS, distinguished from the Separatists . . . 38, 44
    first presbytery of, formed 45
    character and influence of 45

RALEIGH, Sir Walter, plans of, for colonizing America . . 109
ROANOKE COLONY, sketch of 110
ROBINSON, John, account of conversion of . . . 137
    second pastor of Scrooby church 141
    arrival of, in Leyden 166
    place of residence of, in Leyden 167
    counsels of, to the Pilgrims 169
    opinion of the Leyden church 172
    feelings of, toward the church of England . . 173

INDEX.

ROBINSON, John, Hoornbeck's opinion of 178
    names of children of 196
    handwriting of, lost 203
    Fast sermon of 208
    farewell sermon of, to the Pilgrims 244
    final letter of, to the Pilgrims at Southampton . . . 248
ROUGH, John, pastor of a church in London 13

SAGADAHOC COLONY, failure of 230
SAMOSET visits the Pilgrims at Plymouth 272
SANDYS, Sir Edwin, helper of the Pilgrims . . . 205, 228
SCROOBY, situation of 147
    church formed 141
        meet at Brewster's 141
        persecutions of 147
SEPARATISTS, martyrdom of 13
    Archbishop Grindal's description of 14
    names of, imprisoned 15
    first church of 16–19
    why called Brownists 32, 41
    wherein differed from Puritans . . . 38, 44
    weakness of 48
    secret meetings of 49
    plan for prison visitation of 62
    at Southwark, choose church officers 71
    death of, in prison 76
    first petition of, to remove to America 113
    letters of, in prison, how written 117
    first arrival of, in Amsterdam 134
    discussions of, with Francis Junius . . . 135
SLAVERY first introduced into America . . . 279
    English agency in fostering 288
SMYTH, John, forms a society, or church . . . 137
    influence of the writings of 137, 139, 140
    discussion of, with Richard Bernard 140
    letter of, to the church in Scrooby . . . 142
    pastor of church in Amsterdam 163
    peculiar views of 164
SOUTHWARK, church in, organized 71
        officers of, chosen 72
        first communion of . . . 74

SOUTHWARK, church in, members of, arrested	75, 185
deaths of members of	76, 132
reorganized	187
Henry Jacob, pastor of	188
John Lothrop, pastor of	191
attempts of, to build a "Memorial Church"	192
members of, remove to Plymouth	273
SOUTHWORTH, Edward, residence of	203
SPEEDWELL sails from Delft Haven	245
Southampton	251
puts into Dartmouth	252
miserable condition of	253
left at Plymouth	253
STARESMORE, Sabine, agent of the Pilgrims	204
imprisoned	207
THACKER, Elias, arrested and put to death	31
THORP, William, Brownist printer in Holland	211
THURSDAY PRAYER-MEETING, observance of	18
UNIFORMITY ACT of Elizabeth	6
remonstrances against	6
methods of enforcing	8
examinations under	10
VIRGINIA COMPANY, failure of colonies of	230
patent of, given to John Wincob	233
VOLUNTARY SYSTEM, early practice of	6
early doctrine of the	61
WESTON, agent, visits the Pilgrims at Southampton	246
WHITE, William, examination of	20
letter of, to Deering	23
WINCOB, John, holds the Plymouth patent	233
WINTHROP, Hon. R. C., on the Jamestown and Plymouth colonies	274
WRIGHT, Robert, invited to pastorate of Rochford church	52
imprisoned	53
subscription of	53

www.ingramcontent.com/pod-product-compliance
Lightning Source LLC
Chambersburg PA
CBHW021153230426
43667CB00006B/370